# HORACE BUSHNELL

# American Academy of Religion
# Studies in Religion
edited by
Charley Hardwick
James O. Duke

# HORACE BUSHNELL
## Selected Writings on Language, Religion, and American Culture

David L. Smith, Editor

Scholars Press
Chico, California

# HORACE BUSHNELL
## Selected Writings on Language, Religion, and American Culture

David L. Smith, Editor

© 1984
The American Academy of Religion

285.8092
B 979h

**Library of Congress Cataloging in Publication Data**

Bushnell, Horace, 1802–1876
Horace Bushnell, selected writings on language, religion, and American culture.

(Studies in religion / American Academy of Religion ; ISSN 0145–2789 ; no. 33)
Bibliography: p.
1. Theology—Addresses, essays, lectures. I. Smith, David L. (David Lester) II. Title. III. Series: Studies in religion (American Academy of Religion) ; no. 33.
BR85.B9325  1984    285.8'092'4           83–6678
ISBN 0–89130–636–6

Printed in the United States of America

*For Joy, without whom, not.*

Special thanks to the library of
Yale Divinity School for permission to include
previously unpublished portions of "Revelation."

METHODIST COLLEGE LIBRARY
Fayetteville, N. C.

086533

# CONTENTS

# INTRODUCTION

To me the converging objects of the universe
    perpetually flow,
All are written to me, and I must get
    what the writing means.
                                        —Walt Whitman

i

In the summer of 1850, Horace Bushnell was nearly tried for heresy by the associated Congregational churches of Connecticut. A ministerial conference from the western end of the state insisted that his most recent book, *God in Christ*, contained views of the trinity, the incarnation, and the atonement which were "captivating to the carnal mind, but destructive of the faith and ruinous of the souls of men."[1] On the whole, the conservative Calvinist press of New England agreed. Most reviewers found something in the book to offend them, whether it was Bushnell's theological novelty and seeming disregard for tradition ("he is like a man who would leave the ark to ride out the deluge on a slimey log,")[2] or the unfamiliar note of romanticism in his style. So, in 1850, a serious call went forth to bring this "chartered libertine" to trial.[3] The call echoed through four years of debate and procedural infighting, but thanks to the loyalty of Bushnell's congregation, his own personal charm, and (certainly not least) his training in law, the charge of heresy was never made to stick. Bushnell was left in peace to continue teaching what many had judged to be a shocking mixture of "Rationalism, Mysticism and the new Philosophy"—a seductive half-way house on the road to Transcendentalism.[4]

No one reading *God in Christ* today would be likely to suspect that this little episode ever occurred. Bushnell's style, once reputedly incomprehensible, now seems conventional and rather bland. Moreover, his

---

[1] "Remonstrance and Complaint to the Hartford Central Association" from the Association of Fairfield West, quoted in Mary B. Cheney, *Life and Letters of Horace Bushnell* (New York: Harper and Brothers, 1880; rpt. New York: Arno Press, Inc., 1969), p. 234.

[2] Charles Hodge, "Review of *God in Christ*," *Biblical Repository and Princeton Review*, XXI (1849), p. 298.

[3] Comment from the *Puritan Recorder*, quoted in Cheney, *Life and Letters*, p. 226.

[4] The quote is from Hodge, *op. cit.*, p. 264. For a review of the entire "Bushnell controversy," see Cheney, *Life and Letters*, pp. 211–346 and H. Shelton Smith, ed., *Horace Bushnell* (New York: Oxford University Press, 1965), pp. 152–159.

doctrines will not seem at all out of the way to anyone acquainted with the history of modern Protestant thought. Bushnell taught, for instance, that the Bible should be read and responded to as a piece of poetry; that religion is a power that works primarily in and through the human imagination; that supernatural influences, available as sunlight, pervade the organic networks of nature and human society; that the study of language, and especially a sensitivity to the role of metaphor in thought, can provide keys to both human nature and the relation of mankind to the sacred. All of these notions remain remarkably current, though by now they are more than a little shop-worn. Indeed, the main difficulty for a reader of Bushnell today may lie in recovering the freshness of once-powerful ideas that have become almost numbingly familiar.

What's more, it took considerably less than the full span from his day to our own to wear the rough edges off Bushnell's image. By the time of his death, twenty-seven years after the publication of *God in Christ*, Bushnell was revered as a major spokesman for Victorian Protestantism; his published sermons sold well; he was a renowned orator; he was loved as gracefully aging celebrities are loved. By the turn of the century, he was hailed by liberals, modernists, and social gospelers as a forerunner of the epochal transformations of theology they believed themselves to be carrying forward.[5] And today, his reputation seems to be firmly established as the "father of American religious liberalism."[6]

So, what was all the fuss about in 1850? Part of the answer has to do with the highly charged, contentious theological climate of Bushnell's age. The early nineteenth century in New England marked the popular climax of a transformation of American Protestantism that had been preparing for over a century. The older schools of Calvinism, stressing God's terrible justice and absolute sovereignty over against mankind's total depravity, were giving way to teachings stressing a loving God's rational moral government of the universe and mankind's freedom within it. As in any period of intellectual revolution, controversies were rampant and the passions of the disputants ran high. Though the young Bushnell had no taste for extended polemics, he was nevertheless adventurous and ambitious enough to be willing to step into the lines of fire. Thus, he often found himself in the midst of controversies already in progress, and sometimes even in a position to be hailed as a champion of the new liberal ethos. H. Shelton Smith has ably surveyed Bushnell's

---

[5] Eulogies for Bushnell from varying perspectives are collected in *Bushnell Centenary* (Hartford: Hartford Press, The Case, Lockwood and Brainard Co., 1902). The articles by Williston Walker and Theodore Munger are of particular interest. See also Munger's enthusiastic biography of Bushnell, *Horace Bushnell: Preacher and Theologian* (Boston: Houghton, Mifflin and Co., 1889).

[6] Sydney E. Ahlstrom, ed., *Theology in America* (Indianapolis: Bobbs-Merrill, 1967), p. 64.

relationship to three specific debates of the day: the Taylor-Tyler controversy regarding freedom of the will and the means of grace; the Unitarian controversy regarding the doctrines of the trinity and the atonement; and the challenge to orthodox supernaturalism posed by Transcendentalist intuitionism.[7] I will touch on all these questions again in what follows. For now, however, suffice it to say that much of Bushnell's notoriety was inadvertent. He avoided controversy where he could, and when passions surrounding technical questions of theology died down later in the century, he simply ceased to seem dangerous.

A more significant reason for the shifts in Bushnell's reputation lies deeper in the intellectual currents of his age. The following recorded dialogue indicates the issues at stake. It seems that when Bushnell encountered criticism, his typical response was to insist, in effect, that the world was not yet ready for him. A friend recalled confronting him over this uncharacteristic bit of arrogance. "'Why is it,' said I, 'that you complain that you are so generally misunderstood? Where you are criticized you say that the critics misapprehend your positions; and they reply that you ought to express yourself more clearly. Why can you not do so?'" Bushnell answered with an anecdote:

> 'When I was in college I once undertook to read Coleridge's "Aids to Reflection." But the author seemed foggy and unintelligible, and I closed the book, and put it upon my bookshelves, where it remained a long time. Meanwhile, my mind went on thinking and maturing; and one day, my eye falling on the book, I took it down and began to read, and, behold, all was lucid and instructive! And so it will be some time with my writings. Men will read them, and give me credit for perspicuity instead of vagueness and uncertainty. That will be when they have truer conceptions of the soul and of language.'[8]

According to Bushnell, then, his writings would not be likely to become popular or even intelligible until some fairly radical changes had occurred in the intellectual climate—changes affecting our foundational views of the human psyche, of language, and "'of the relation of language to spiritual truth.'"[9] If we accept Bushnell's diagnosis of the situation, it follows that his popularity in later life is a signal that some such transformation had in fact occurred. And if Bushnell's works still strike modern readers as "familiar"—part of "our" intellectual world in the way that, say, the works of Francis Bacon are and those of Roger Bacon are not—then it is because we are still part of the age or discursive environment that Bushnell helped to initiate.

I am inclined to take Bushnell at his word. Indeed, I think that the

---

[7] H. Shelton Smith, ed., *Horace Bushnell*, pp. 3–39.
[8] William Patton, quoted in Cheney, *Life and Letters*, pp. 207–8.
[9] *Ibid.*

best reason for reading Bushnell today is that he can be taken as a kind of "representative man" of modern humanistic thought, a pioneer of certain views of "the soul and of language" that still have an astonishingly wide cultural diffusion. For example, like many modern students of literature, philosophy, and religion, Bushnell explored metaphor and polysemous symbolism for clues to the depths of human nature and the limits of human knowing; like much modern psychology, he stressed the indeterminacy and the ineffability of the inward life of the psyche, and the consequent need for artful interpretation of its ambiguous expressions; and like most modern theologians, his approach to theology was "relational," always seeking the grounds for religious knowledge in human consciousness and experience. It is not possible to say that Bushnell was a unique influence or even a major force in establishing these views in the modern world. In all these respects, his work drew on and ran parallel to the more seminal writings of Coleridge, Schleiermacher, and the romantics generally. Nevertheless, he gave these ideas a clear, engaging voice and assembled them into an elegant whole centered on the concepts of expression and communication. His work is thus at once original and thoroughly representative. At its best, it is alive with intellectual tension and a sense of discovery. A study of Bushnell, then, can provide a reader with a small but refreshingly clear window on modern Western thought and spirituality in the making, a sort of re-introduction to the age—whatever its name—in which we still live, move, and carry on our conversations.

ii

The best-worn path into Bushnell's work leads by way of his life. For example, his most insightful biographer, Barbara Cross, portrays him as "minister to a changing America," showing in detail how his work was shaped by the social transformations of nineteenth century New England as well as by his more purely theological concerns.[10] However, too singleminded an attempt to correlate Bushnell's thought with his life might cause us to miss the inner structuring that gives the work its significance and drive. Bushnell is not only a representative of his times; he is the creator of a powerful vision of divine-human relations that merits attention in its own right. Therefore, after a look at Bushnell's life and times, I will go on to sketch the central themes of Bushnell's work more systematically.

Bushnell was born in rural Litchfield County, Connecticut, in 1802. His family's small wool carding and weaving business provided him with

---

[10] Barbara Cross, *Horace Bushnell: Minister to a Changing America* (Chicago: University of Chicago Press, 1958).

the homespun clothing he wore until age twenty-five and the only ambitions he cherished for himself until age nineteen. As eldest son, he intended to become his father's apprentice. However, his mother had other plans. She wanted Horace to go to college and take up what then seemed a sure route to social prestige for a country boy: a career in the ministry. But young Bushnell's attitude toward established religion was, if anything, hostile. He felt intellectually uncomfortable with Calvinism, nurturing instead a rationalistic impulse, as he put it, to "dig out a religion by my head."[11] In adolescence, he may even have belonged to a local "infidel club" lead by a "hard headed Deist of the type of Paine."[12] In any case, he had little to do with the local Congregational church until the early 1820s, when the development of large-scale textile manufacturing in New England brought a decline in the market for homespun, a rise in Bushnell's anxieties about the future, and a not entirely coincidental rise in the tenor of his religious experience. In 1822 he joined the local church and the following year he entered Yale.[13]

In college, however, his main concerns were social rather than religious. He longed to connect with the great world of learning and polite society that his rural background had done so little to prepare him for. Characteristically, he saw his situation as a language problem.

> I entered college late,—at twenty-one years of age, when the vernacular type of language is cast and will not afterwards commonly be much altered. I came to writing with no stock of speech but this. I had no language, and if I chanced to have an idea, nothing came to give it expression. The problem was, in fact, from that point onward, how to get a language, and where.[14]

After college, his quest for a vocation and an effective language led him successively into school teaching, journalism, and ultimately back to Yale for law school. But Bushnell did not really find his voice until, in 1831, he was again caught up in a season of religious enthusiasm. Yale was stirred that year by one of the religious awakenings that periodically swept Connecticut throughout the 1820s and 30s.[15] At first, Bushnell held aloof from the general fervor. But something in him—Bushnell called it his "heart"— was irresistably drawn to the evangelical ethos. His "head" might resist, but ultimately his sentimental attachments prevailed. "'What shall I do with

11 Cheney, *Life and Letters*, p. 32.
12 See Noah Porter, "Horace Bushnell, A Memorial Sermon," *The New Englander*, XXXVI (1877), p. 159.
13 The best sources for Bushnell's early life are Cheney, *Life and Letters*, pp. 3-66; and Cross, *op. cit.*, pp. 1–20.
14 Cheney, *Life and Letters*, p. 208.
15 See Charles Roy Keller, *The Second Great Awakening in Connecticut*, (New Haven: Yale University Press, 1942).

these arrant doubts I have been nursing for years?'" he reportedly sighed at
a Yale prayer meeting.

> 'When the preacher touches the Trinity and when logic shatters
> it to pieces, I am all at the four winds. But I am glad I have a
> heart as well as a head. . . . My heart says the Bible has a Trinity
> for me, and I mean to hold by my heart. I am glad a man can do
> it when there is no other mooring. . . .'[16]

So, as it happened, his mother's ambitions for him were finally to be fulfilled. His Christian convictions renewed, Bushnell entered Yale Divinity
School the following term with an evident sense of relief that his
vocational meandering was over.[17]

   A number of conversations were in progress at the Divinity School
when Bushnell stepped into its classrooms, many of which would shape
his language for the rest of his career. The dominant voice in the school
at the time was Nathaniel William Taylor, theological bulldog of the
second great awakening in New England. While another teacher later
recalled Bushnell as having been "t' other side" of every important issue
from Taylor,[18] Taylor's mark on his student is nonetheless clear. Above
all, Taylor's teaching convinced Bushnell once and for all of the truth
and theological relevance of the Scottish "Common Sense" school of
philosophy—the then-dominant ideology of American higher education.
The most important feature of this philosophy for the story at hand is its
moral and epistemological intuitionism, carefully hedged but powerfully
suggestive. The existence of things in themselves and the principles of
right and wrong were held to be immediately knowable or intuitively
available to the "common sense" of mankind. Moreover, the moral laws
thus built into "the very nature and structure of the mind,"[19] were identical with the moral order established in creation by God. A thinker
discovering a moral law, or for that matter any law of the created order,
was "thinking God's thoughts after him;" he was penetrating the secrets
of the divine nature as expressed in creation. Thus, the moral sense of
mankind, however errant it had become in practice, was in principle a
mirror of the mind and moral being of God. And thus Bushnell came
easily to speak of

> the grand analogy, or almost identity that subsists between our
> moral nature and that of God; so that our moral pathologies and
> those of God make faithful answer to each other, and He is
> brought so close to us that almost any thing that occurs in the

[16] Robert McEwan, quoted in Cheney, *Life and Letters*, p. 56.
[17] *Ibid.*, p. 33.
[18] *Ibid.*, p. 62.
[19] Nathaniel Taylor, *Lectures on the Moral Government of God* (New York: Clark,
Austin and Smith, 1859), vol. I, p. 200.

working or exigencies of our moral instincts may even be expected in His.[20]

The main theological implication of this philosophy, then, was to lessen the distance between mankind and the divine. Clearly, as a way of thinking about divine-human relations, it left little room for an infinite qualitative distinction between God and man; it even tended to undercut classical Calvinism's doctrine of man's total depravity, his unlikeness to God. On the contrary, human nature was held to be, in principle, a reliable index to the divine nature and to the objective moral truths that organize the universe.

Taylor's most controversial inference from the Scottish philosophy concerned the freedom of the human will in the process of religious conversion. New England theology had long been divided between strict predestinarians like Jonathan Edwards and his followers, who held that fallen persons can neither will nor do anything to bring about their own salvation, and on the other hand, the liberal "Arminians," who held that persons can freely choose whether or not to accept God's grace. Taylor brought the resources of the Scottish philosophy to the Arminian side. Against predestinarianism, he argued that it is the universal intuition of mankind that our will is under our own control; after all, if it were not, we could not justly be held responsible for our acts. Now, said Taylor, the Bible makes it clear that God *does* hold us responsible for our acts, with eternities of misery to pay. Therefore, it must be the case that God, the just judge of our deserts, made us free and fully able to choose for ourselves between right and wrong, salvation and damnation. Any other view of the matter would make God an arbitrary tyrant. But any theology that makes God vicious is morally repugnant, and what runs counter to the moral sense cannot be true of God. Therefore, Taylor concluded, a loving God upholds human freedom.[21]

Old Lights like Bennet Tyler of East Windsor, Taylor's most most vociferous opponent, objected that the essence of classical Calvinism—the vision of God's sublime sovereignty—had utterly evaporated from Taylor's formulas. Most Americans, however, seemed not to care. Taylor's theology told them what they were already eager to hear. The trend throughout early nineteenth century America was to reduce the theoretical distances

[20] Bushnell, *Forgiveness and Law* (New York: Scribner, Armstrong and Co., 1874; rpt. Hicksville, New York: The Regina Press, 1974), p. 35. On the Scottish philosophy and its influence in America, see especially D.H. Meyer, *The Instructed Conscience* (Philadelphia: University of Pennsylvania Press, 1972); Sidney Mead, *Nathaniel William Taylor, 1786-1858* (Chicago: University of Chicago Press, 1942); and Sydney Ahlstrom, "The Scottish Philosophy and American Theology," *Church History*, XXIV (1955), pp. 257-72.
[21] The most readily available piece of writing by Taylor is his, "Concio ad Clerum," in Ahlstrom, ed., *Theology in America*, pp. 213-49. On Taylor's moral philosophy, see also Mead, *op. cit.*

between God and humanity, God and the world. The notions of mankind's freedom, likeness to God, and moral ability were winning ready acceptance across all lines of class and geography, from backwoods Methodism to Boston Unitarianism. Thus, Bushnell, aligning himself with the thought of his teacher, was also in step with the spirit of the age. Religious thought was to take its cues from the "common sense" of its audience, in more senses than one. "If we must have a philosophy," Bushnell declared while still a student at the divinity school, "let it be one such as reveals itself in the spontaneous, we may almost say unconscious movements of the spirit. There is no other; and that is religion, Christianity itself."[22]

Taylor's use of moral philosophy as a touchstone for theological reasoning was thus a formative influence on Bushnell at Yale. Another such influence, milder but no less decisive, came through Bushnell's training in philology under Josiah Willard Gibbs, Sr.[23] Gibbs was one of the early practitioners of the "higher" Biblical criticism in America, but it was not this aspect of his work that attracted Bushnell. (Bushnell, in fact, was remarkably unimpressed by the new historical/critical approaches to Scripture that so profoundly challenged many of his contemporaries. His interpretations of the Bible were never sophisticated in the modern sense.)[24] Instead, it was Gibbs' general theory of language that captivated Bushnell's imagination. According to Gibbs, all words (beyond a narrow category of nouns referring to sensible objects and mathematical ideas) are metaphorical.

> Words which originally belonged to the world of sense, and denoted sensible objects, operations, and relations, are transfered, by a metaphor depending on a perceived analogy, to the world of intellect to express mental objects, operations, and relations.[25]

Thus, for instance, "spirit" is etymologically related to the word for breath; "comprehension" to physical grasping; and so on. In fact, said Gibbs, every word referring to the "world of intellect" can be traced back to a physical image.

Gibbs was content simply to observe these etymological relations and to suggest that many puzzles of Biblical interpretation could be solved by taking them into account. Bushnell, however, quickly leapt beyond

[22] Bushnell, "Natural Science and Moral Philosophy," MS Yale Divinity School.
[23] On Gibbs and his influence on Bushnell, see Jerry Wayne Brown, *The Rise of Biblical Criticism in America* (Middletown, Conn.: Wesleyan University Press, 1969), pp. 171–79.
[24] See for instance Bushnell's comments on Strauss's Biblical criticism in *Nature and the Supernatural* (New York: Charles Scribner, 1858; rpt. New York: AMS Press, 1973), pp. 22–23.
[25] Josiah Willard Gibbs, Sr., *Philological Studies*, (New Haven: Durie and Peck, 1857), p. 15.

his teacher and turned these observations into a metaphysic. If all the terms of intellect can be built out of words of physical reference, Bushnell reasoned, then there must be some way in which the things used as images are *appropriate* to the thoughts they carry. Meditating, perhaps, on Gibbs' notion of a "perceived analogy," he concluded that physical objects must have been created specifically to serve as vehicles for our thought. How else could one account for the mysterious felicity with which natural objects lend themselves to become the objective correlatives of our thoughts, the readiness with which "the external grammar of creation answers to the internal grammar of the soul, and becomes its vehicle."[26] How else could we be able to express our inner lives by means of physical images and be understood?

In these speculations, Bushnell found support in several perennial traditions in Western thought which speak of relations of "analogy" or "correspondence" between the physical world, the mind of God, and human minds: e.g., Platonism, Logos philosophy, typology, and the Rennaissance master-image of the universe as God's book, to name just a few. His thought jumbles these traditions promiscuously, but the theory he derived from them nevertheless comes across with visionary clarity. "There is a logos in the form of things," he wrote in *God in Christ*,

> by which [physical objects] are prepared to serve as types or images of what is inmost in our souls. . . . And if the outer world is the vast dictionary and grammar of thought we speak of, then it is also itself an organ throughout of Intelligence. Whose intelligence? By this question we are set directly confronting God, the universal Author. . . .[27]

Mankind, nature, and God, in other words, are woven together in one web, and the term that relates them all is language. Bushnell's theory of language thus snowballed into a comprehensive vision of divine-human relations—a vision strikingly similar to Emerson's metaphysic of language.[28] Gibbs would not have appreciated the result, but it seems to have been his teaching that supplied the seed.

Finally, an extra-curricular influence on Bushnell also deserves mention: the religious and critical writings of Samuel Taylor Coleridge. Bushnell probably became acquainted with this notoriously "difficult"

---

26 Bushnell, *God in Christ* (Hartford: Brown and Parsons, 1849; rpt. New York: AMS Press, 1972), p. 28.

27 *Ibid.*, p. 30. On the intellectual backgrounds of Bushnell's theory of symbolism, see especially Donald Crosby, *Horace Bushnell's Theory of Language* (The Hague: Mouton, 1975); and David L. Smith, *Symbolism and Growth* (Chico, California: Scholars Press, 1981), pp. 5–22.

28 See especially the section on "Language" in Emerson's "Nature": *Nature, Addresses and Lectures*, Robert Spiller and Alfred Ferguson, eds. (Cambridge: The Belknap Press of Harvard University Press, 1979), pp. 17–23.

author soon after James Marsh's popular American edition of the *Aids to Reflection* was published in 1829. Understanding was slow in dawning, but once it came, Bushnell's sense of intellectual kinship with Coleridge grew to the point where, late in life, he was reported to say that "he was more indebted to Coleridge than to any extra-Scriptural author."[29]

"Indebted" may be too strong a word. Bushnell was too self-reliant a scholar to systematically appropriate anyone's work. In fact, he once said of his reading habits, "it is hard for me to read a book through. . . . If it is really worth reading, it starts my mind off on some track of its own that I am more inclined to follow than to find out what the author has to say."[30] Even with this caveat in mind, however, it is certainly safe to say that Bushnell's thinking was aided and abetted by Coleridge on several crucial points.

First, the two shared a sense of the divine as a power that "abides" in the world, or of nature and the supernatural as interpenetrating realities. As Coleridge put it,

> there is something in the human mind that makes it know (as soon as it is sufficiently awakened to reflect on its own thoughts and notices), that in all finite quantity there is an infinite, in all measure of time an eternal; that the later are the basis, the substance, the true and abiding reality of the former. . . .[31]

Bushnell's similar sense of the spiritual significance of "finite quantity" is apparent in his views on the metaphorical significance of the physical world.

Second, both men saw *language* as the key to understanding this organic interrelationship of God, mankind, and the world. On the one hand, language was taken to be an appropriate image of the God-world relation. Nature was the "language" of God, the means by which He expresses Himself to other minds. On the other hand, this idea of nature as God's language was immediately borrowed back to provide a model for understanding the nature and limits of human language. As nature expresses God, but is by no means identical with Him, so human language expresses the spirit of man, but in metaphorical terms which are in no sense the literal equivalents of the inner states they express.[32] Our words can suggest the reality of the inner life, but can never capture or exhaust it. In both human speech and divine creation, then, the spiritual

---

[29] Cheney, *Life and Letters*, p. 499.

[30] *Ibid.*, p. 295.

[31] Samuel Taylor Coleridge, *Aids to Reflection* (4th London edition, 1840; rpt. Port Washington, New York: Kennikat Press, 1971) p. 131. Precisely similar definitions of nature and the supernatural are given by Coleridge and Bushnell respectively in *Aids to Reflection*, pp. 108n, 110, 236; and *Nature and the Supernatural*, pp. 36–37.

[32] See Coleridge, *Aids to Reflection*, pp. 62–63. Numerous illustrations of Bushnell's view are included in what follows.

realities are primary. Language—whether consisting of words as for men or of objects and events as for God—plays a secondary, utilitarian role as the vehicle through which spirit is made known and by means of which alone it can be communicated.

Lastly, both Bushnell and Coleridge developed attitudes toward religious doctrines and creeds corresponding to their views of language. Both took it as a first principle that language cannot represent the inward spirit of mankind or God precisely; it can only suggest the spirit by image and metaphor. Precision in theology or any other science of the spirit is thus an unrealizable ideal. For, as Bushnell wrote,

> And what is theology? It is commonly supposed to be a speculated system of doctrine, drawn out in propositions that are clear of all metaphor and are stated in terms that have finally obtained a literal and exact sense. But no such system is possible, for the very plain reason that we have no such terms.[33]

Accordingly, theologians should leave off wrangling about the precise meaning of terms and acknowledge that creeds are poems and theologies fabrics of images directing us to truths of the spirit in the only way they can: by indirection. The skills theologians should cultivate are not argumentative and logical but poetic, for as Bushnell put it, "poets . . . are the true metaphysicians."[34] Similarly, just as both Bushnell and Coleridge held that the forms of language are secondary in importance to the inward states they represent, so both held that the real stuff of religion is experience, not doctrine. Christianity, said Coleridge, is "not a theory, or a speculation; but a life. . . ."[35] Therefore creeds need never be taken with ultimate seriousness, as if religious truth depended on them. Religious truth, in fact, cannot be defined at all; it can only be lived. Theological language, then, is never to be thought of as more than a tool for the cultivation and communication of soul.

When Bushnell left Yale in 1832, then, he carried considerable intellectual freight with him: the Scottish moral philosophy; a nascent vision of the interpenetration of God, nature, and mankind; and a theory of language that inclined him to view all theological positions as tools more or less helpful in the development of spiritual character. When he took over the ministry of the North Church of Hartford, Connecticut, later that same year, all of these views were immediately put to the test. The church was in turmoil, evenly divided against itself over the issue of free will already familiar to Bushnell from Nathaniel Taylor's classrooms. Half of the congregation adhered to Edwardsian predestinarianism, half

---

[33] Bushnell, "Our Gospel a Gift to the Imagination", in *Building Eras in Religion* (New York: Charles Scribners Sons, 1881), p. 268.

[34] Bushnell, *God in Christ*, p. 73.

[35] Coleridge, *Aids to Reflection*, p. 201.

to Taylor's doctrine of moral ability. Bushnell, feeling like a plate "daintily inserted between an acid and an alkali," sought to secure the middle ground.[36] Because both the question at issue and Bushnell's way of dealing with it typify the patterns of his thought throughout his career, I will examine the situation in some detail.

What was at stake in this debate, as Bushnell saw it, was more than the question of human freedom. The real issue lay between two different views of how God is related to the world, and thus, of how mankind can come into relation to sacred power. The predestinarian Calvinists in his congregation stressed God's distance from the world and difference from mankind. Fallen or "natural" persons were held to be drastically alienated from the divine life. Practically speaking, then, a supernatural act on God's part was required to bring persons back into a living relation with God: a miracle, a special revelation, or, more familiarly, an inward experience of saving grace, as in revivalistic conversion. Without some such eruption of the divine into history—some sharp break with the continuities of natural life—a right relation to God was impossible. By contrast, the free will party asserted a smoother continuity between the divine and the human realms. Taylor, for instance, had argued that any person could be saved who freely and sincerely willed to be so. Grace was available; it was part of the moral environment of "natural" or unconverted persons. All they had to do was to avail themselves of it. But, as some thinkers were beginning to see, if this was so, then the line between nature and grace becomes perilously fine. Grace is domesticated to the point that it becomes a potential implicit in natural life itself. Christian character becomes no more than a development of human nature. Taylor himself refused to embrace these naturalistic conclusions, but contemporary radicals like Theodore Parker were soon to be drawing them enthusiastically from largely similar premises.[37] And so, on the far horizon of the free will debate lay the momentous question whether human spirituality required a naturalistic or a supernaturalistic interpretation.

Characteristically, Bushnell saw value in both sides of the dispute, even when it was cast in these radical terms. Accordingly, he devised a view of the matter designed to "comprehend" or include the truths of the conflicting doctrines (a tactic that he later developed into a general program for "Christian comprehensiveness"[38]). It is true, said Bushnell in

---

[36] Bushnell, *Twentieth Anniversary: A Commerorative Discourse* (Hartford: Elihu Geer, 1853) p. 8. Most of the theological issues of Bushnell's career are described concisely in this pamphlet.

[37] See Theodore Parker, "A Discourse of the Transient and the Permanent in Christianity," in Perry Miller, ed., *The Transcendentalists* (Cambridge: Harvard University Press, 1950), pp. 259–83.

[38] On Bushnell's preference for a "comprehensive" strategy in resolving theological disputes, see Bushnell, "Christian Comprehensiveness," *The New Englander* VI (1848), pp.

an early sermon to his divided congregation, that God's self-communication is required to set a person's spirit right; supernaturalism is right to this extent. But it is also true that God's presence in the world is abiding and ubiquitous. God is "in-resident in his works;" spirit is an "air-medium, common, or present, both to the divine mind and to ours."[39] What is needed to turn this presence into a power is simply a person's free acceptance of it. Mankind, then, is dependent on God, but only in the sense that a seed is dependent on water and sunlight for its growth. Grace is necessary to transform fallen persons, but the transformation is accomplished by means of an abiding supernatural presence at the heart of nature.

Bushnell's church found this quite acceptable. The Edwardsians recognized their characteristic doctrine of mankind's total dependence on God; the Taylorites approved the stipulation that persons can and must assert their own wills. Bushnell thus came through the challenge gratified to find his native inclinations certified by success, and with the germ of his "comprehensive" theological method "experimentally proved."[40]

Bushnell's popularity with his Hartford congregation became so well established, in fact, that he was able to hold his position there for the rest of his public life. From the first, however, he knew that the role of pastor would not be enough to satisfy his ambitions. The New England clergyman's social power was no longer what it had been before disestablishment, and Bushnell longed to be influential.[41] Therefore he experimented with a number of alternative projects throughout the 1830s and 40s. He spoke out on presidential politics, on slavery, and on the social problems created by Irish immigration; he traveled to London as a representative of an anti-Catholic, Protestant ecumenical association, the Evangelical Alliance; most memorably, he wrote widely against revivalism and in support of a gradualist interpretation of Christian nurture. As might be expected, his illiberal polemics against "Romanism" and the dangers of Western "barbarism" won him immediate fame. His writings on Christian education, on the other hand, won him some sharp criticism from the religious press.

Bushnell's writings on "Christian nurture" are basically in line with the position we have already seen him adopting on the free will issue.

81–111, reprinted in *Building Eras in Religion*; and Irving Bartlett, "Bushnell, Cousin, and Comprehensive Christianity," *Journal of Religion*, XXXVII (1957), pp. 99–104.

[39] See "Duty Not Measured by Our Own Ability," written in 1833 and published in *Sermons for the New Life* (New York: Charles Scribner, 1858), p. 372. See also "The Spiritual Economy of Revivals of Religion" (1838), in *Views of Christian Nurture* (1847; rpt. Delmar, New York: Scholars Facsimiles and Reprints, 1975), pp. 126f, 129.

[40] Bushnell, *Twentieth Anniversary*, p. 14.

[41] On the social malaise of New England clergymen in the early nineteenth century, see Ann Douglas, *The Femininization of American Culture* (New York: Alfred A. Knopf, 1977), pp. 17–43.

Again, the central question in Bushnell's mind was the nature of divine-human relations. Revivalists (who, in Bushnell's Connecticut, were frequently predestinarians) held that a special, rather drastic experience of conversion was necessary to set a person right before God. These saving relations between the soul and God were conceived to be wholly individual and mainly restricted to persons who had reached the age of reason. Bushnell, by contrast, held that the energies of grace were "in-resident" and available in ordinary experience, and preeminently so in the atmosphere of a Christian household. Therefore children could and should be expected to grow up in grace from their earliest years. Far from being hardened in sin from birth, children, according to Bushnell's social psychology, are "passive lumps;" they take on the image of any type of character they are exposed to in their formative years.[42] All that is really necessary for their salvation, then, is a pair of sincere Christian parents—embodiments of the Christian spirit—who, as "living epistles," will naturally communicate that spirit to their children through every detail of life. As words express inward states, so every word, deed, and gesture of a Christian person will express and communicate the substance of Christian consciousness. Thus, Bushnell affirmed that Christian character can flow from parent to child "just as naturally and by a law as truly organic, as when the sap of a trunk flows into a limb." Grace, as the energy of a renewed life, was communicable through the same social channels that shape natural human identity.[43]

Conservative reviewers of the "Discourses on Christian Nurture" (1847) replied that this was heretical naturalism, pure and simple. If no special, supernatural act of God is required to bring about salvation, they asked, then what need has man of God? Bushnell replied with injured puzzlement that he had always assumed his position to be orthodox, and that of course, a supernatural act was required to make grace available to mankind—namely, the incarnation. But now that Christ *has* come and the secret of a divine character has been shown forth in human terms, the energies of the divine life can be communicated through the ordinary channels of human social interaction. Grace has interpenetrated the world insofar as the world has become "Christianized."[44]

Bushnell, in short, refused to alter his stance. He continued to worry over the question of the proper relations of nature and the supernatural

---

[42] Bushnell, *Views of Christian Nurture*, p. 19.

[43] *Ibid.*, pp. 19, 200.

[44] See Bushnell, "Argument for 'Discourses on Christian Nurture'" in *Views of Christian Nurture*, pp. 49–121. To my knowledge, Bushnell uses the verb "to Christianize"—later to become a central term of the social gospel movement—only in the address "How to Be a Christian in Trade," published in *Sermons on Living Subjects* (New York: Scribner, Armstrong and Co., 1872) pp. 264–65. The general concept, however, runs through all his writings.

for several years, eventually expanding his reflections into a major treatise. The title of that work, however, simply sums up the vision of
divine-human relations he had held from the beginning: *Nature and the
Supernatural As Together Constituting the One System of God*
(1858).[45]

For all his intellectual intransigence, Bushnell was rather badly
shaken by the harsh critical response to his "Discourses." His health
declined; his self-confidence suffered; he sought inward renewal in the
mystical piety of Quietism. Then, in February of 1848, came a decisive
turning point in his career. Late one night, as his wife reports, he had a
powerfully moving spiritual experience, a "personal discovery of Christ,"
we are told, which reinforced his "'sense of the freeness of God and the
ease of approach to him'" and initiated an unparalleled burst of literary
creativity.[46] The addresses comprising *God in Christ* were all written
and delivered that same year; the "Preliminary Dissertation on the
Nature of Language" was composed, giving mature expression at last to
the language-centered metaphysic he had nurtured since seminary and
providing the key to all his subsequent theological work. Whatever the
experience may have been, and whatever forces were set in motion by it,
its effect was clearly to crystalize Bushnell's sense of vocation. In 1848,
he became what he would remain for the rest of his life: from his own
point of view, an inspired spokesman for a complex vision of "the relation of language to spiritual truth"; from the literary historian's point of
view, a representative American Victorian man of letters.

We have already seen how *God in Christ*, the first-fruit of his
insight of 1848, was received. The cry of heresy was raised. What aggra-
vated reviewers seems primarily to have been Bushnell's relativistic attitude toward creeds and theological formulas. As we have seen, Bushnell
held that creeds are no more than imprecise, metaphorical suggestions of
an interior, spiritual truth, and therefore that "all formulas of doctrine
should be held in a certain spirit of accommodation. They cannot be
pressed to the letter, for the very sufficient reason that the letter is never
true."[47] In *God in Christ*, he argued moreover that all the Christian
creeds are really more or less clumsy attempts to point to the same truth:

when they are subjected to the deepest chemistry of thought, that

---

[45] Because Bushnell's "One System" insisted that human growth and well-being are
dependent on special acts of divine self-revelation, it was not quite in tune with the more
self-reliant "natural supernaturalism" that M. H. Abrams has identified at the heart of the
romantic intellectual project. Nevertheless, Bushnell consistently taught a "supernatural
naturalism" that discovered resources of sacred power within the natural order while
acknowledging their transcendent source. See M.H. Abrams, *Natural Supernaturalism*
(New York: W. W. Norton and Co., Inc., 1971).

[46] Cheney, *Life and Letters*, pp. 192–93.

[47] Bushnell, *God in Christ*, p. 81.

> which descends to the point of relationship between the form of
> the truth and its interior formless nature, they become, there-
> upon, so elastic, and run so freely into each other, that one sel-
> dom need have any difficulty in accepting as many as are offered
> him.[48]

In an age when religious seriousness was virtually identified with doctri-
nal precision, Bushnell's relativism seemed like mere capriciousness, or
even worse, insincerity. Few at the time suspected that Bushnell's determination to pierce beneath the surface of creedal formulas to the spirit
they expressed represented a quest for sincerity of another sort—the
romantic urge to bring spirit into the immediate presence of spirit, dis-
solving all merely external differences in the "deepest chemistry of
thought." Bushnell's message could not be received until his age developed a new conception of truthfulness, or until its conception of "the
relation of language to spiritual truth" allowed it to perceive truth in
contradictions.

That day was not long in coming. For several years, however, Bushnell found himself *persona non grata* at professional meetings; he was
refused the common fellowship of pulpit exchanges. Not surprisingly, he
became depressed. He complained of feeling possessed by an "angel of
dryness" and turned temporarily from theology to a deeper involvement
in pastoral work.[49] He even tried his hand at city planning, providing
the design and the political impetus for the Hartford city park, now
called Bushnell Park—a milestone in American landscape architecture.
His health, marred since the 1830s by a vaguely tubercular lung disease,
became even more troublesome. He traveled widely in his quest for
recovery, most notably to California, where he picked out and surveyed
the site for the new University of California at Berkeley.

At home in Hartford, his health continued to decline. The persistent
weakness of his lungs led him to resign his position at the North Church
in 1859. In the meantime, however, his wider reputation had flourished
and his self-confidence had recovered completely. Time, it turned out,
was on his side in intellectual and cultural matters. The tempest raised
by *God in Christ* had come to seem almost laughably anachronistic in
the light of the cultural transformations of the Civil War era. The more
dynamic pluralism of American life made Bushnell's quest for unity
beneath a variety of forms seem timely. Thus a growing reading public
helped make the years after his retirement some of his most productive
in literary terms. Indeed, the remainder of his life, until his death in
1876, is mainly the history of a quick succession of books applying his
theological vision to contemporary social topics—from the Civil War to

---

[48] *Ibid.*, p. 82.
[49] Cheney, *Life and Letters*, p. 251–52.

women's suffrage—and to the re-interpretation of classical Christian doctrines, especially the doctrine of the atonement.

Bushnell was so "successful" in later life, in fact, that he virtually disappears into the stereotypic acclaim that surrounded him. The memoires and studies that began appearing soon after his death cast him in any number of roles according to the preferences of various audiences. We see him portrayed, for instance, as an honest son of the land by patriotic moralists; an intellectual pioneer by liberal theologians; a man of exquisite sentiment by representatives of a "feminized" mass culture.[50] By the turn of the century, many prominent churchmen, including Walter Rauschenbusch, Washington Gladden, Theodore Munger, and Josiah Strong, were proud to place themselves in his lineage. But almost to the same extent that his achievement was absorbed into the mainstream, he ceased to be taken seriously. He was warmly praised as "one of us" by spokesmen for the progressive middle class, but he was seldom engaged critically.[51]

The heart of Bushnell's achievement, however, was his theological vision. And this, in several senses, had no history: first, because it went largely unappreciated by his followers; second, because in the context of Bushnell's own life it was formed early on and remained constant in outline throughout the vicissitudes of his career. Therefore, in order to return to what is really essential to Bushnell, it will be necessary to shift from narrative to a brief introduction to the structure of Bushnell's thought.

### iii

Bushnell's theology is primarily an inquiry into how religion—Christianity in particular—becomes a transforming power in human life. How does sacred power enter a human community, and how does it become a shaping influence in the lives of individuals? His answer, in its most general form, is that divine energies enter the world as "language" through all the forms of God's self-expression.

> What is the Christian truth? Pre-eminently and principally, it is the expression of God—God coming into expression, through histories and rites, through an incarnation, and through language—in one syllable, by the Word. The endeavor is, by means of

---

[50] For a representative collection of Bushnelliana, see *Bushnell Centenary*. Other contemporary reminiscences are listed in the bibliography appended to Bushnell, *The Spirit in Man* (New York: Charles Scribner's Sons, 1903), pp. 468–73.

[51] Notable exceptions to this rule are the insightful articles by Williston Walker in *Bushnell Centenary*, pp. 15–34; and George B. Stevens, "The Theology of Horace Bushnell," *Methodist Review* LXXXIV (1902), pp. 692–707.

> expression, and under the laws of expression, to set forth God—
> . . . God's own feeling. His truth, love, justice, compassion.[52]

The divine self-expression becomes a transformative power, in turn, whenever the divine nature is "read," understood, and appropriated by a receptive imagination. Forms of self-expression have a power to communicate the life they represent, Bushnell believed. Therefore Christianity, as divine self-expression, reaches its end in the communication of the divine nature.

> I should like . . . to use the word *esthetic*, and represent Christianity as a power moving upon man, through this department of his nature, both to regenerate his degraded perception of excellence, and also to communicate, in that way, the fullness and beauty of God.[53]

The place of the terms "language" and "expression" in Bushnell's thought should already be apparent. But to see clearly how language—human or divine—can be capable of transforming human character, we need to look more closely at Bushnell's notion of understanding, or of what happens when language is interpreted. Put as simply as possible, if language is a matter of *ex*-pressing inner states, then understanding involves receiving their *im*-pression.[54] To understand, in fact, is to re-experience the experiential content expressed in a metaphoric vehicle. It is to feel, in an only slightly distanced way, what the communicating party feels; to know what he or she knows; or to see what he or she sees. Ultimately this means that any act of communication results in the *communion* of the communicating parties, in that understanding another person's expressions involves recapitulating his or her inner states. Consequently, to understand another mind, one must have a sympathetic capacity or ground of potential experience of a sort that allows one to relive the other's experience in one's own mind. In short, understanding presupposes the likeness of the communicating parties.

When this analysis of understanding is applied to communications between human minds, its implications are familiar enough. The theory is part of the stock in trade of romantic hermeneutics as that tradition has passed from Schleiermacher to Dilthey to Bultmann and Betti.[55] When the same analysis is applied to communications between human

---

[52] Bushnell, *God in Christ*, p. 74.

[53] *Ibid.*, p. 204.

[54] See Bushnell, "Unconscious Influence," in *Sermons for the New Life*, p. 192.

[55] The parallels between Bushnell and Dilthey on the nature of understanding are especially clear. For a brief, general introduction to this school of hermeneutic theory, see Josef Bleicher, *Contemporary Hermeneutics* (Boston: Routledge and Kegan Paul, 1980) pp. 11-94. I differ from Bleicher in stressing Bultmann's connection with the "classical" lineage.

minds and the mind of God, however, the implications may be surprising. Most of what once appeared novel and still appears fresh in Bushnell's theology, in fact, stems from his consistent application of this model of communication to the interpretation of divine-human relations.

For instance, as we have already noted, Bushnell viewed everything that exists as God's expression or self-communication. Various aspects of creation communicate the divine with different degrees of intensity. Nature is a rather general and vague form of revelation. Scripture and the providential history it recounts are more specific and intentional. The person of Christ, as "God's last metaphor,"[56] is revelation at its most concentrated and pure. But all is revelation. The whole world is a "hieroglyph" whose solution is the being of God.

It follows, then, that the primary task of religious life is to become a right reader of the revelation that has been made; spiritual life is by definition a hermeneutic process.[57] In order to become right interpreters, persons must first get into a position to receive the communication of the divine nature, and so, enter into communion with God. But obviously, there is a catch. To receive God's communication, one must already be able to recapitulate a divine inwardness in one's own character. Understanding entails likeness of mind. Mankind is fallen, however, and the significance of the fall is precisely alienation from the divine life, alienation from the conditions of understanding. So, if mankind is ever to be able to interpret God's self-revelation and so regain a divine character, help is necessary. And to this end, God initiated the history of salvation. All the events of Biblical history, culminating in the incarnation, are artful means by which God has educated and manipulated mankind back into a position where persons can receive the divine self-revelation made in Christ. By drilling mankind in the law, God prepares them to comprehend the gospel; through threats and promises that appeal to our lower nature, we are maneuvered into a position where we are at least able to recognize our own higher nature when it is revealed in the face of Christ.[58] To be a Christian, in sum, is to have received the benefit of these "lessons of history" and so to have become a right interpreter of creation.

The parallel between Bushnell's understanding of divine-human communication and Jonathan Edwards' theory of the "sense of the heart" is striking, especially so because Bushnell, like most latter-day New England theologians, was not particularly sensitive to this aspect of

---

56 Bushnell, "Our Gospel a Gift to the Imagination," in *Building Eras in Religion*, p. 259.
57 On the role of a "right sensibility" in spiritual life, see *God in Christ*, p. 302; also "Our Gospel," in *Building Eras in Religion*, p. 266.
58 Bushnell gives his fullest accounts of the providential education of the race in *Nature and the Supernatural* and in *The Vicarious Sacrifice* (New York: Charles Scribner and Co., 1866; rpt. Hicksville, New York: The Regina Press, 1974).

Edwards' work. Both men affirmed that the *sine qua non* of spiritual life is the ability to see the divine nature expressed as beauty. Likewise, both stressed the correlation between this ability and the inward condition of the believer's heart or character. The principal difference between them is, in effect, the difference between their predestinarian and Arminian estimates of human nature. Edwards saw the sense of the heart as a special dispensation of grace given only to the elect. Bushnell, by contrast, saw sensibility to the divine nature as a potentially universal human capacity, dependent only on a right education to bring it out. One could say, then, that Bushnell democratized Edwards' sense of the heart.[59]

That this is so becomes clear when we turn to Bushnell's views on the nature of Christian social influence. Because the incarnation brought the divine life into contact with mankind in an especially compelling way, said Bushnell, the whole communicative situation of man in the world is changed. Christ, being divine, perfectly embodied the divine character, which is also the norm of human moral character. As a man among men, he communicated himself socially to his followers through all the ordinary human channels of word, deed, and gesture. What he expressed to those who understood him, however, was extraordinary. It was no less than the divine life itself. His followers, through social communion with him, came to recapitulate his divine inwardness and so became Christian characters, Christs to their neighbors, capable of communicating his divine life to others. Thus, the life of God entered the stream of the world's life; a "divine contagion" began to spread.[60] Larger and larger portions of society became "Christianized" as they became spheres for the expression of Christian character. In short, the world had become one in which "Christian nurture" was possible. The energies of grace—the energies of a divine life—had become available through ordinary interpersonal channels insofar as the persons involved partook of the character first lived into the world by Christ.

All of Bushnell's theological positions are easily comprehensible with reference to this scheme. His general opposition to logical rigor as an ideal in theology, for instance, stems from his conviction that Christian life is primarily a discipline in the interpretation of symbols. Words, as symbols, cannot literally represent truth, he wrote, nor can they literally convey it from one mind to another.

They are only hints or images, held up before the mind of

---

[59] For a brief, helpful discussion of Edwards on the sense of the heart, see John E. Smith, ed., *Religious Affections* by Jonathan Edwards, (New Haven: Yale University Press, 1959), esp. pp. 8–27. See also Edwards' own discussion in the same volume, esp. pp. 205–6.

[60] Bushnell, *Forgiveness and Law*, p. 153.

another, to put *him* on generating or reproducing the same
thought; which he can do only as he has the same personal contents, or the generative power out of which to bring the thought
required.[61]

Accordingly, theologians should learn to view the imagination rather
than the reason as their primary instrument for setting forth Christian
truth. Or, as he put it elsewhere, by an inward realization of God, theologians should learn to practice *divinity* rather than mere theology.[62]

It follows also from this view of the role of language in Christian life
that a paradox or contradictory statement may be a better instrument for
conveying truth than a straightforward proposition: "as form battles
form, and one form neutralizes another, all the insufficiencies of words
are filled out, the contrarieties liquidated, and the mind settles into a full
and just apprehension of pure spiritual truth."[63] Accordingly, Bushnell
held that the Bible is intentionally, artfully chocked full of contradictions, precisely in order to "drive our minds to the Infinite," beyond the
insufficiencies of form. The primary mysteries of Christianity—the trinity and the incarnation—are blunt paradoxes. "They offer God, not so
much to the reason, or logical understanding, as to the imagination and
the perceptive, or esthetic apprehension of faith. Then, also, their contrarious, or logically insoluble matter is to be handled in the same way,
as that of all language, when applied to thought."[64] Similarly, he held,
the atonement is represented in Scripture under a wide range of
images—ransom, sacrifice, vicarious offering, propitiation—and these
representations, all in tension with each other, are effective in communicating truth precisely *because* they are contradictory.

Finally, as we have seen, Bushnell's doctrine of Christian nurture and
his broader doctrine of the systematic interrelation of nature and the supernatural trace back to his idea of natural forms as metaphorical vehicles for
the communication of spirit. Thanks to the self-communication of God in
Christ, the spirit of God now interpenetrates the world in the same way
that "spirit" or meaning interpenetrates the letter in verbal communication. Grace, the energy of a divine life, can now be communicated through
ordinary interpersonal relations—one Life, manifested by God in Christ,
received by Christians, and manifested or communicated by them in turn
through ever-widening circles of influence.

Inevitably, all of the least attractive aspects of Bushnell's work can
also be traced back to his vision of the realized interrelations of God,
mankind, and nature. His characteristic fault, we might say, is the sin

---

[61] Bushnell, *God in Christ*, p. 46.
[62] See Bushnell, *Christ in Theology*, p. 80ff.
[63] Bushnell, *God in Christ*, p. 55.
[64] *Ibid.*, p. 102.

most likely to beset any thinker who believes that the sacred is closely interwoven with the profane: that is, he was often rather too quick to assume that the "Christianization" of society had already been accomplished, and too ready to believe that the character of the Christians he knew was virtually identical with the divine self-hood of Christ. It is not that Bushnell had too little regard for human evil. On the contrary, his conception of the tragic solidarity of the race in sin—of sin as an infection of the organic channels of interpersonal communication—is one of the most powerful and most lasting emphases of his theology.[65] The problem is rather that Bushnell simply had too high a regard for Victorian morality. The moral intuitions his philosophy invited him to take as the hallmarks of divine character turn out to be very much the virtues of his time and place. Bushnell's praise of domesticity, his distrust of immigrant cultures, his repressive idealization of "feminine character" and consequent opposition to women's suffrage, his tendency to identify the progress of American empire with the progress of Christianity—all these make Bushnell very much a man of his own time and emphatically not one of ours.

If we are less ready today to identify the city of man with the city of God, however, we may still be receptive to the motives that sometimes drove Bushnell to make the identification. Bushnell, like many writers from the romantic era to our own, sought to record the epiphanies of sacred power still available to mankind in a largely desacralized world and to discern what he could of pure Presence in the increasingly obscure media of modern life. We may no longer find our signals of transcendence in the same places Bushnell did, but we may be no less likely to feel the urgency of the quest.

iv

For this volume, Bushnell's writings have been edited and organized to show how his specific theological and social views emerge from a more basic set of assumptions regarding language and its role in spiritual life. The reader is therefore introduced to Bushnell's opus by way of his writings on symbolism and communication. These are not only the aspects of his work most likely to interest a modern reader; they are also, as many commentators have noted, "the key" to his entire cast of mind.[66] No attempt is made, then, to give a complete representation of the technical complexity and refinement of his theology. Instead, I concentrate on works and passages that will help to make the whole of his

---

[65] Bushnell develops his views on the organic solidarity of the race in sin in *Nature and the Supernatural*. His view of the matter is substantially identical with that of Walter Rauschenbusch in *A Theology for the Social Gospel* (1917).

[66] See Cheney, *Life and Letters*, p. 203.

thought intelligible, indicating the wider range of his work by means of just a few important examples. Serious students of theology or American history can and should then go on to his more detailed works, many of which are readily available today in reprints.[67]

Briefly then: Part I, "Language and Doctrine," will introduce Bushnell's theory of language and show how the theory shaped his general view of the theological task and his specific interpretations of the incarnation and the trinity. Part II, "The New Life," will show how his views on language were set within a larger theory of interpersonal communication, according to which language serves as the key to the "discipline of life." Here are included selections from his various writings on the means and ends of Christian growth: especially his theories of the atonement and of Christian nurture. Finally, Part III, "Social Studies," will present writings in which Bushnell brought his vision to bear on contemporary social topics: women's suffrage, the "Christianization" of society, Westward expansion, and the Civil War. Short introductions to each part will provide further information on the specific selections included.

[67] See the Selected Bibliography at the end of this volume.

# PART I

# LANGUAGE AND DOCTRINE

# I. LANGUAGE AND DOCTRINE

[I]f it were possible to get religious truth into shapes and formulas having an absolute meaning, like the terms of algebra, as clear even to the wicked as to the pure, and requiring no conditions of character in the receivers, it would very nearly subvert, it seems to me, all that is most significant and sublime in the discipline of life.

—Bushnell, *Christ in Theology*

Bushnell's writings on language and symbolism are, in effect, an extended commentary on the above quote—an attempt to account for the close relationship he perceived between the metaphorical character of language and the "discipline of life." He first combined his theory of language as an expressive or poetic vehicle of mind with his view of religious life as a process of interpreting the self-expression of God in an address titled "Revelation," delivered to the Porter Rhetorical Society of Andover Theological Seminary in 1839. The essay was hastily prepared, and Bushnell never bothered to rework in for publication. Nevertheless, he felt even at the time that by discussing human speech and divine self-expression under the one heading of "revelation," and by interpreting both in terms of the same "laws of expression," he was taking a new departure in theology that was as revolutionary and possibly as consequential as Luther's. (See Mary Bushnell Cheney, *The Life and Letters of Horace Bushnell* [New York: Harper and Brothers, 1880], pp. 88–90.) The selections from "Revelation" included here are previously unpublished.

Other selections grouped under the heading "The Theory of Language" include the bulk of the "Preliminary Dissertation" to *God in Christ* (1849), which contains not only Bushnell's most complete statement on the nature of language and the sources of its power, but also some of his finest prose. Next come selections from *Christ in Theology* (1851), a book written to answer the charges of theological irregularity that were leveled at Bushnell after the publication of *God in Christ*. As should be apparent, however, Bushnell retracted none of his former positions on language in this sequel. On the contrary, he went on to sharpen his distinction between logical and figurative language, and moved to the conclusion that authentic theology (or "divinity") must be a commentary on the contents of Christian consciousness, or on what is received by an attentive and well-tempered imagination from God's metaphorical self-expression.

Under the heading "The Wording Forth of God" are included writings in which Bushnell made use of his understanding of the means and ends of self-expression to reinterpret the classical Christian doctrines of incarnation and trinity. The first three selections from *God in Christ* and *Christ in Theology* show how Bushnell developed his basic approach to these doctrines out of his theory of language. Both the dual nature of Christ and the triune nature of God are presented simply as forms required by God to express his own complex unity to finite minds; they are metaphoric tools for what Bushnell himself refers to as "the wording forth of God." Thus, as Bushnell put it in a later work, "Our Gospel a Gift to the Imagination" (1864), there is no better way to speak of the incarnate Christ than as "God's last metaphor." In "The Christian Trinity a Practical Truth" (1854), Bushnell modified his views on the trinity to allow for the eternal inherence of trinity in the divine nature. However, he never altered his original understanding of trinity and incarnation as instrumental forms necessitated by God's plan to relate himself expressively to creation.

# THE THEORY OF LANGUAGE
## From "Revelation" (1839)*

The highest aspect of grandeur in God is beheld not in his knowledge or in his power but in his publicity. . . . Not the Bible only reveals him but the whole temple of being around us and above is written over with spiritual hieroglyphs all radiant with his light.† If this grand system of exposure were taken only as a proof that he shrinks from no inspections or that he can justify his integrity to the universe, the contrast of his open conscience with the hiding reserve and guiltiness of men would move us with awe. But it is a wider and holier revelation—a publicity whose task is condescension—a publicity whose object is to communicate to creatures that which is their life—the warmth, light, beauty, and truth of the Divine Nature.

I propose at this time to offer you some thoughts on this interesting subject of revelation. . . . The fundamental idea of revelation (I speak of revelation in the general) is that it brings truth into outward exhibition, or into some one of the forms of the senses. It does not create truth, for truth exists before it is revealed and is revealed because it exists. It does not deduce truth but offers it to simple inspection. Argument or logic, the office of which is only to show that some proposition is involved in some other, presupposes revelation followed by an act of simple inspection in which the truth of that proposition has been seen. Revelation is further distinguished from history or a narrative of facts. A revelation may be made by means of facts and narratives or through them but it will yet be no more identical with them than are the letters in which truth is written with truth itself.

The word revelation always contemplates this one fact—that truth is in her nature invisible, having in herself neither color, shape, voice, nor tangibility and therefore capable of being communicated only by some manifestation or apparition which presents her to view. Thus . . . [i]n producing a revelation of truth there are two great conditions which are indispensable.

* [Ed.] MS Yale Divinity School Library. The selections printed here are from pp. 1–32 of the manuscript. Excerpts from the final pages of the address are printed in Bushnell, *The Spirit in Man* (New York: Charles Scribner's Sons, 1910), pp. 357–59.

† [Ed.] For the historical context and cultural significance of Bushnell's reference to "hieroglyphs" here, see John Irwin, *American Hieroglyphics: The Symbol of Egyptian Hieroglyphics in theAmerican Renaissance* (New Haven: Yale University Press, 1980).

First Condition. There must be forms provided which are fit to be the signs or outward bodies of truth. The truth-world having no form, a form-world must be constituted to be its mirror. There must be just so many bodies of truth as there are truths to be bodied, each one having a look or a voice or a touch that reveals it or makes apparition of it. I use the word *form* in this connection somewhat scholastically as related to all the senses, not the sight and touch only. If we had not used the words image and metaphor in a sense so unreasonably limited by the masters or rhetoric, I might say that every truth must have its image or metaphor whereby it may be shown. Or if I should say that every truth must have its type, I should mean the same thing.

Second Condition. That the beings to whom revelation is to be made have intelligence to read the forms set forth and ascend to the truth intended by them. A revelation could not be made to animals because they live in their senses only and never ascend to a metaphorical signification beyond sense. But man is a creature so quickened by the divine principle of intelligence that he feels the mysterious analogy between forms and truths and darts through one to the other scarcely conscious of the transition. An ox gazing on the burning bush would have seen all that Moses saw, or hearing the still small voice would have heard as much as Elijah the prophet, but it would have been a fire in his eye or a whisper in his ear, not the type of an invisible God. And in this you see that a revelation never conveys truth from one mind to another; it only holds out some image which puts the beholder on generating for himself the thought intended which he does out of his own sagacity quickened by the image presented. . . .

Observe the beautiful provision of God for this object. Having his eye fixed on this necessity of man he has constructed the outward world (i.e. our body and the realm of nature around us) so as to furnish a vast store house of types or images fitted to represent thoughts and be interpreted between man and man. The whole outward world in its objects, colors, scenes, sounds, motions, wants, and the like is analogical to thought and truth and constitutes in the whole a grand system of figure work spiritually significant. . . .

I stand here then a thinking creature in a vast temple of being. The sky is over me, the earth is beneath, and around me I gaze on the floor and the walls and the shafted pillars of the temple and behold all overlaid and inlaid with types of thought. Whose thought? If I am intelligent so is the world. I live here—amazing thought!—embosomed in the eternal intelligence of God. As David expresses it and perhaps with more than David's meaning I repeat—The heavens declare the glory of God and the firmament showeth his handy work. Day unto day uttereth speech and night unto night showeth forth knowledge. There is no speech nor language where their voice is not heard. Or as a living poet

sublimely expresses it—In these eloquent signs of intelligence around me
I read the Eternal deep Forever haunted by the Eternal mind.*

In a word I behold God. I arrive at him by no deduction of logic
rising from design to designer or from effect to cause, which if it move
me at all drives me up on an eternal series of Gods. He is revealed to
me. I see him with a direct gaze of simple inspection as I see any man
through his bodily types of look and action. Here then in language we
have a revelation of God which shows as in a mirror one vast and varied
image of his intelligence.

* [Ed.] The Biblical passage is Psalm 19:1-3. The "living poet" is William Wordsworth,
and the quotation is a rough rendition of "Intimations of Immortality from Recollections
of Early Childhood," lines 113-114.

From *God in Christ,*

## "Preliminary Dissertation on the Nature of Language as Related to Thought and Spirit" (1849)*

The subject of which I speak, is language; a very different instrument, certainly, from what most men think it to be, and one, which if they understood more exactly, they would use more wisely. In the misuse or abuse of this instrument, a great part of our religious difficulties have their spring. We have misconceived, as it seems to me, both its nature and its capacities, and our moral reasonings are, to just the same extent, infected with error. Indeed, it is such an instrument, that I see not how any one, who rightly conceives its nature, can hope any longer to produce in it a real and proper system of dogmatic truth. He will doubt the capacity of language to serve any such purpose. He will also suspect that our logical or deductive processes under it, are more likely, in general, to be false than true. And yet, in the matter of Christian doctrine, or Christian theology, we are found committing ourselves most unsuspectingly to language and logic, as if the instrument were sufficient, and the method infallible.

I do not propose, in the dissertation that follows, to undertake a full investigation of language. I freely acknowledge my incompetence to any such undertaking. What I design is, principally, to speak of language as regards its significancy, or the power and capacity of its words, taken as vehicles of thought and of spiritual truth. What I may offer concerning other topics involved in the general subject, such as the origin of language; the phonology of words, or the reason why certain things are named by certain sounds, and not by others; letters and the written forms of words; laws of grammar; questions of ethnology, and the like; will be advanced in a purely incidental way, and with no other design than to make my theory of the *significance* of words more intelligible and clear. I cannot promise that I shall fall into no mistakes which the learned philologists and grammarians will detect, though I have little fear that they will discover any important error in what I advance, in regard to the philosophy of words, taken as *instruments of thought,*

* [Ed.] *God in Christ* (Hartford: Brown and Parsons, 1849), pp. 9–117. Included here: pp. 11–13, 18–26, 30–50, 55–91.

which is the particular subject under discussion.

To understand the precise power of words, or the true theory of their power, without some reference to their origin, will be difficult or impossible; for it is, in fact, the mode of their origin that reveals their power. And yet what we say of their power may be true, in general, if what we say of their origin should not hold in every particular. . . .

We suppose, then, two human persons to be thrown together, who, as yet, have never heard the use of words, and, of course, have no language. Considered simply as human, they have a certain ground or preparation in their very nature for speech. In one view, language is in them potentially beforehand, only it is not developed into actual existence; they are linguistic natures, so to speak, only it is not yet clear what kind of tongue they are going to create. This, in fact, is the opinion of Humboldt, and also of many of the most competent philologists. "Speech," he says, "according to my fullest conviction, must really be considered as inherent in man: language could not have been invented without its type pre-existing in man."* This being true, we are then to see it formed or developed afterward, and become a historical fact. As to the manner in which the process goes on, I find no conception of it given which is satisfactory, or which adequately explains a universal fact pertaining to the significance and power of language, as an instrument of thought and spiritual expression.

There is no difficulty in perceiving how our two unlanguaged men will proceed, when thrown together in the manner supposed, as far as the naming of sensations of physical objects is concerned. For the object is always present as a mediator or interpreter between them, so that when a sound is uttered as a name for it, or in connection with it, they may always know to what the sound or name refers. Thus all sights, sounds, smells, tastes, and touches, or feelings, or what is the same, their objects, are easily named, and their names will come into currency without difficulty, when sounded as representatives of the objects. As to the sounds adopted, they will generally be determined arbitrarily, or, at least, by causes so occult or remote that we must regard them as arbitrary. . . .

We have now seen how our two language-makers will get on, in the naming of things or physical objects. In this manner they will make out a string of *nouns* or names, which may be called a noun-language. It will comprise the names of all physical objects and demonstrations,

* [Ed.] Wilhelm von Humbolt (1767–1835), German philologist, noted for the thesis that the structure of a language expresses the inner life of those who speak it. H. Shelton Smith traces the passage to Humbolt's "Uber das vergleichende Sprachstudiems" of 1822. (See Smith, *Horace Bushnell* [New York: Oxford University Press, 1965], p. 74.) However, Bushnell spoke no German, and I have been unable to identify a probable source for his English version.

including, of course, the names of actions; for verbs, prior to the formation of grammar, are only the nouns or names of actions. Thus far we
have generated only a physical language, or terms of physical import.
And thus far, even, animals are capable of language: they can learn,
though not as easily and on as large a scale as we, to associate names or
sounds with outward things and actions.

There now remains to be formed another sphere of language, wholly
distinct, which the animals cannot learn, viz.: the language of intelligence; that which, under an outward form, carries an inward sense, and
so avails to serve the uses of mind. It has been easy for our language-
makers to agree in the use of sounds standing for outward objects and
acts, because these outward objects and acts can be so fixed upon, or the
mind so directed towards them, that a mutual understanding may be
had in regard to the object which it is designed to name, before the
name to be adopted is uttered. But if, now, one of them has a thought or
emotion in his mind, or wishes to speak of a spiritual being or world,
this, it will be seen, is not capable of being shown or pointed at, because
it lies out of sense. The thought or emotion cannot be taken out and
exhibited to the eye: how, then, can the two parties come to any such
understanding as will enable them to name it? Here is a difficulty, and it
is the great difficulty to be surmounted, in the production of intellectual
language. And if we are to understand the nature of language as an
instrument of thought and spiritual truth, or to judge of its capacity for
uses of this kind, it will be just here, in the solution of this difficulty
relating to the genesis of language, that we shall get the desired key to
its significance in such uses.

How, then, shall our experimenters proceed? Obviously they cannot
advance at all, save through the mediation of things; that is, of objects
and acts in the sensible world, which may come in to their aid as signs of
thought, or interpreters between them. It is only as there is a Logos in
the outward world, answering to the logos or internal reason of the
parties, that they can come into a mutual understanding in regard to any
thought or spiritual state whatever. To use a more familiar expression,
there is a vast analogy in things, which prepares them, as forms, to be
signs or figures of thoughts, and thus, bases or types of words. Our bodily
mechanism, and the sensible world we live in, are, in fact, made up of
words, to represent our thoughts and internal states;—they only want
naming, and then, passing into sound, to be re-produced or have their
images called up by sounds, they drop out, so to speak, their gross material quality, and become words of spirit, or what the poet calls "winged
words;"—cursitating forms of life, that fly out in sound upon the air, as
interpreters and messengers of thought between the minds of men.

Thus, if the mind of one of our two strangers is laboring with any
thought or emotion, he will strike at some image or figure in the sensible

world, that is itself a fit representation of his thought or emotion—a form prepared in nature to be its type. Turning the attention of the other party upon this image, and signifying by gesture, probably, that he is trying to mirror some internal state in it, he puts the other party on generating that internal state, or the conception of it. The image becomes, in fact, a common sign or conception of the same internal state—they understand each other. So that, now, the name, when it is sounded, will stand, not merely as the name of the object or image physically taken, but the name, also, of that thought which it represented. And thus an intellectual word is generated. . . .

We find, then, that every language contains two distinct departments:—the physical department—that which provides names for things; and the intellectual department—that which provides names for thought and spirit. In the former, names are simple representatives of things, which even the animals may learn. In the latter, the names of things are used as representatives of thought, and cannot, therefore, be learned, save by beings of intelligence—(*intus lego*)—that is, beings who can read the inner sense, or receive the inner contents of words; beings in whom the Logos of the creation finds a correspondent logos, or reason, to receive and employ the types it offers, in their true power.

For the benefit of the mere English reader, who is wholly unexercised in subjects of this nature, it may be important to say, that what is here advanced in theory, is fully supported by reference to the actual history of our words. We cannot always, or in every instance, show what physical object or act lies named in our intellectual words to give them their power; though in a great majority of cases, the words carry their origin in their face; and where they do not, it is only to be supposed that the physical history of the word or name is lost.

Thus, the word *spirit* means, originally, *breath*, or air in motion; that being the symbol, in nature, of a power moving unseen.

The word *religion* is *re*, back, and *ligo*, to bind—the conception being that man is made to be free, but bound back in terms of obligation to his Maker.

In the same manner, *expectation* is a looking forth, and *hope* a reaching forth, in which we see how accurately the original physical meaning of the word governs and distinguishes the internal meaning; for we look out for [expect] the coming of things both good and bad, but reach after [hope for] only those that we desire.

In the same way we have *prefer*, to set before; *abstraction*, drawing apart; *reflection*, turning back; *obedience*, before-hearing, as when a servant stands before his master, listening to receive his commands; *glory*, brightness; *grace*, outward beauty or concinnity; *faith*, a tie or ligature; *right*, straight.

Or sometimes a word takes a historical origin. Thus, the word *sincerity* is supposed to be the same as *sine*, without, and *cera*, wax; the practice of the Roman potters being, to rub wax into the flaws of their unsound vessels when they sent them to market. A sincere [without-wax] vessel was the same as a sound vessel, one that had no disguised flaw.*

The English reader is to understand that all the terms in language, which are devoted to spiritual and intellectual uses, have a physical or outward sign underlying their import, as in the cases here named. Of this the scholar has never a doubt, although he cannot always, or in every instance, trace out the physical sign or base of the word, so as to be certain of it. All things out of sense get their names in language through signs and objects in sense that have some mysterious correspondence or analogy, by which they are prepared beforehand to serve as signs or vehicles of the spiritual things to be expressed. . . .

In this view . . . the outer world is seen to be a vast menstruum of thought or intelligence. There is a logos in the forms of things, by which they are prepared to serve as types or images of what is inmost in our souls; and then there is a logos also of construction in the relations of space, the position, qualities, connections, and predicates of things, by which they are framed into grammar. In one word, the outer world, which envelops our being, is itself language, the power of all language. Day unto day uttereth speech, and night unto night showeth knowledge; there is no speech nor language where their voice is not heard,—their line is gone out through all the earth, and their words to the end of the world.†

And if the outer world is the vast dictionary and grammar of thought we speak of, then it is also itself an organ throughout of Intelligence. Whose intelligence? By this question we are set directly confronting God, the universal Author, no more to hunt for Him by curious arguments and subtle deductions, if haply we may find Him; but He stands EXPRESSED every where, so that, turn whichsoever way we please, we behold the outlooking of His intelligence. No series of Bridgewater treatises, piled even to the moon, could give a proof of God so immediate, complete, and conclusive.‡

---

* [Ed.] Bushnell's views on etymology derive from the work of Josiah Willard Gibbs, Sr., under whom he studied at Yale Divinity School. For a similar view of the history of words and even a similar catalogue of examples, see Gibbs, *Philological Studies* (New Haven: Durrie and Peck, 1857), pp. 14–15. On the relationship between Bushnell and Gibbs, see Jerry Wayne Brown, *The Rise of Biblical Criticism in America, 1800–1870* (Middletown: Wesleyan University Press, 1969), pp. 171–79.

† [Ed.] Psalm 19:2–4.

‡ [Ed.] Francis Henry Egerton, Earl of Bridgewater (1756–1829), established an endowment to fund studies in natural theology which, like William Paley's *Natural Theology* (1802), would demonstrate the "Power, Wisdom, and Goodness of God as manifested in

In such a view of the world, too, and its objects, there is an amazing fund of inspiration elsewhere not to be found. The holding of such a view is, in fact, sufficient of itself, to change a man's intellectual capacities and destiny; for it sets him always in the presence of Divine thoughts and meanings; makes even the words he utters luminous of Divinity, and to the same extent, subjects of love and reverence. . . .

We pass now to the application of these views of language, or the power they are entitled to have, in matters of moral and religious inquiry and especially in Christian theology.

There are, as we discover, two languages, in fact, in every language. Or perhaps I shall be understood more exactly, if I say that there are, in every human tongue, two distinct departments. First, there is a literal department, in which sounds are provided as names for physical objects and appearances. Secondly, there is a department of analogy or figure, where physical objects and appearances are named as images of thought or spirit, and the words get their power, as words of thought, through the physical images received into them. Thus, if I speak of my *pen*, I use a word in the first department of language, uttering a sound which stands for the instrument with which I write. But if I speak of the *spirit* of a man, or the *sincerity* of a Christian, I use words that belong to the second department of language, where the sounds do not stand for the mental ideas as being names directly applied to them, but represent, rather, certain images in the physical state, which are the natural figures or analogies of those mental ideas. How it was necessary, in the genesis of language, that it should fall into this twofold distribution, has been shown already. The man who knows his tongue only by vernacular usage, is aware of no such distribution. Many, who are considered to be educated persons, and are truly so, are but half aware of it. At least, they notice only now and then, when speaking of matters pertaining to thought and spirit, that a word brought into use has a physical image in it. For example, when speaking of a good man's *heart*, they observe that the word has a physical image connected with it, or that it names also a vital organ of the body. Then they either say, that the word has two meanings, a physical and a spiritual, not observing any law of order or connection by which the physical becomes the basis or type of the spiritual; or, they raise a distinction between what they call the *literal* and *figurative* uses of the word. But this distinction of literal and figurative, it does not appear to be noticed, even by philologists, runs through the

---

the Creation." One such treatise, well-known in Bushnell's day, was William Kirby's *On the Power, Wisdom and Goodness of God, as Manifested in the Creation of Animals and in Their History, Habits, and Instincts* (2 vols; London: William Pickering, 1835). Bushnell vents his impatience with this whole school of natural theology frequently in his writings.

very body of the language itself, making two departments; one that comprises the terms of sensation, and the other the terms of thought. They notice, in the historical investigation of words, that they are turning up all the while, a subsoil of physical bases; and, though they cannot find in every particular case, the physical term on which the word is built, they attain to a conviction that every word has a physical root, if only it could be found; and yet the natural necessity, that all words relating to thought and spirit should be figures, and as such, get their significance, they do not state. They still retain the impression that some of the terms of thought are literal, and some figurative.

This is the manner of the theologians. They assume that there is a literal terminology in religion as well as a figurative, (as doubtless there is, in reference to matters of outward fact and history, but nowhere else,) and then it is only a part of the same mistake to accept words, not as signs or images, but as absolute measures and equivalents of truth; and so to run themselves, by their argumentations, with a perfectly unsuspecting confidence, into whatever conclusions the *logical forms* of the words will carry them. Hence, in great part, the distractions, the infinite multiplications of opinion, the errors and sects and strifes of the Christian world. We can never come into a settled consent in the truth, until we better understand the nature, capacities and incapacities of language, as a vehicle of truth.

In order, now, that I may excite our younger theologians especially to a new investigation of this subject, as being fundamental, in fact, to the right understanding of religious truth, I will dismiss the free form of dissertation, and set forth, under numerical indications, a series of points or positions inviting each their attention, and likely, though with some modifications, perhaps, to be finally verified.

1. Words of thought and spirit are possible in language only in virtue of the fact that there are forms provided in the world of sense, which are cognate to the mind, and fitted, by reason of some hidden analogy, to represent or express its interior sentiments and thoughts.

2. Words of thought and spirit are, in fact, names of such forms or images existing in the outward or physical state. . . .

5. There are no words, in the physical department of language, that are exact representatives of particular physical things. For whether we take the theory of the Nominalists or the Realists, the words are, in fact, and practically, names only of genera, not of individuals or species. To be even still more exact, they represent only certain sensations of sight, touch, taste, smell, hearing—one or all. Hence the opportunity in language, for endless mistakes and false reasonings, in reference to matters purely physical. This subject was labored some years ago with much

acuteness and industry, by one of our countrymen, Mr. Johnson, in a 'Treatise on Language, or the Relations of Words to Things. . . .'*

6. It follows, that as physical terms are never exact, being only names of genera, much less have we any terms in the spiritual department of language that are exact representatives of thought. For, first, the word here used will be the name only of a genus of physical images. Then, secondly, it will have been applied over to signify a genus of thoughts or sentiments. And now, thirdly, in a particular case, it is drawn out to dignify a specific thought or sentiment which, of course, will have qualities or incidents peculiar to itself. What, now, can steer a word through so many ambiguities and complications, and give it an exact and determinate meaning in the particular use it is applied to serve? Suppose, for example, one desires to speak of the *bitterness* displayed by another, on some given occasion. In the first place, this word *bitterness*, taken physically, describes not a particular sensation common to all men, but a genus of sensations; and as some persons have even a taste for bitter things, it is impossible that the word, taken physically, should not have an endless variety of significations, ranging between disgust and a positive relish of pleasure. If, now, it be taken as the base or type of an intellectual word, it will carry with it, of necessity, as great a variety of associations; associations so unlike, that it will be impossible to clothe it with the same precise import, as a word of sentiment. Then, secondly, men are so different, even good and true men, in their personal temperament, their modes of feeling, reasoning and judging, that moral bitterness, in its generic sense, will not be a state or exercise of the same precise quality in their minds. Some persons will take as bitterness in general, what others will only look upon as faithfulness, or just indignation. And, then, thirdly, in the particular case to which the word is to be applied, different views and judgments will be formed of the man, his provocations, circumstances, duties, and the real import of his words and actions. Accordingly, as one declares that he was bitter, another will receive the declaration as no better than a real slander. And so it must of necessity be. It is impossible so to settle the meaning of this word *bitterness*, as to produce any exact unity of apprehension under it. And the same is true of the great mass of words employed in moral and spiritual uses,—such as love, gentleness, contentment, patience, wisdom, justice, order, pride, charity. We think we have the same ideas in them, or rather, (which is more likely,) we think nothing about it; but we find continually that, when we come to particular uses, we fall into disagreements, often into protracted and serious controversies; and whether it be

* [Ed.] See Alexander Bryan Johnson, *A Treatise on Language, or The Relations of Words to Things* (ed. David Rynin; Berkeley and Los Angeles: University of California Press, 1959), first published in 1836.

said that the controversy is about words or things, it is always a controversy about the real applicability of words.

What, then, it may be asked, is the real and legitimate use of words, when applied to moral subjects? For we cannot dispense with them, and it is uncomfortable to hold them in universal scepticism, as being only instruments of error. Words, then, I answer, are legitimately used as the signs of thoughts to be expressed. They do not literally convey, or pass over a thought out of one mind into another, as we commonly speak of doing. They are only hints, or images, held up before the mind of another, to put *him* on generating or reproducing the same thought; which he can do only as he has the same personal contents, or the generative power out of which to bring the thought required. Hence, there will be different measures of understanding or misunderstanding, according to the capacity or incapacity, the ingenuousness or moral obliquity of the receiving party—even if the communicating party offers only truth, in the best and freshest forms of expression the language provides.

There is only a single class of intellectual words that can be said to have a perfectly determinate significance, viz., those which relate to what are called necessary ideas. They are such as time, space, cause, truth, right, arithmetical numbers, and geometrical figures. Here the names applied, are settled into a perfectly determinate meaning, not by any peculiar virtue in *them*, but by reason of the absolute exactness of the ideas themselves. Time cannot be anything more or less than time; truth cannot, in its idea, be anything different from truth; the numerals suffer no ambiguity of count or measure; a circle must be a circle; a square, a square. As far as language, therefore, has to do with these, it is a perfectly exact algebra of thought, but no farther.

It will, perhaps, be imagined by some, indeed, it is an assumption continually made, that words of thought, though based on mere figures or analogies in their original adoption, gradually lose their indeterminate character, and settle down under the law of use, into a sense so perfectly unambiguous, that they are to be regarded as literal names, and real equivalents of the thoughts they signify. There could not be a greater mistake. For, though the original type, or historic base of the word may pass out of view, so that nothing physical or figurative is any longer suggested by it, still it will be impossible that mere use should have given it an exact meaning, or made it the literal name of any moral or intellectual state. The word *sin* is of this description, and most persons seem to imagine that it names a given act or state, about which there is no diversity of understanding. Contrary to this, no two minds ever had the same impression of it. The whole personal history of every man, his acts, temptations, wants, and repentances; his opinions of God, of law, and of personal freedom; his theory of virtue, his decisions of the question, whether sin is an act, or a state; of the will, or of the heart: in fact, his whole theology and life will enter into his impression of this word *sin*, to change the quality, and modify the relations of that which it signifies. It will also be found, as a matter of fact, that the interminable disputes of the theologians on this particular subject, originate in fundamental differences of view concerning the nature of sin, and are themselves incontestible proofs that, simple as the word is, and on the lips of every body, (as we know it to be) there is yet no virtual agreement of meaning connected with the word. The same, as just now intimated, is true of *hope, fear, love*, and other like familiar terms, which we fancy have a meaning so well settled. They have a dictionary meaning that is settled; but yet, hope, fear, love, is to every man what his own life-experience, and his theories, and mental struggles have made it, and he sees it, of necessity, under a color quite peculiar to himself; so peculiar, that he will even advance concerning it, what another cannot find the truth of, or receive. And this is true of all the intellectual terms in language, with the exception of a class just named, relating to necessary and absolute truths. Besides these, there is no word of thought, or spirit, that exactly measures its ideas, or does any thing more than offer some proximate notion, or shadow of the thought intended. . . .

7. Words of thought or spirit are not only inexact in their significance, never measuring the truth or giving its precise equivalent, but they always affirm something which is false, or contrary to the truth intended. They impute *form* to that which really is out of form. They are related to the truth, only as form to spirit—earthen vessels in which the truth is borne, yet always offering their mere pottery as being the truth itself. Bunyan beautifully represents their insufficiency and earthiness when he says—

> "My dark and cloudy words, they do but hold
> The truth, as cabinets inclose the gold."*

—only it needs to be added that they palm off upon us, too often, their "dark and cloudy" qualities as belonging inherently to the golden truths they are used to express. Therefore, we need always to have it in mind, or in present recollection, that they are but signs, in fact, or images of that which has no shape or sensible quality whatever; a kind of painting, in which the speaker, or the writer, leads on through a gallery of pictures or forms, while we attend him, catching at the thoughts suggested by his forms. In one view, they are all false; for there are no shapes in the truths they represent, and therefore we are to separate continually, and by a most delicate process of art, between the husks of the forms and the pure truths of thought presented in them. We do this insensibly, to a certain extent,

* [Ed.] John Bunyan, *The Pilgrim's Progress*, "The Author's Apology for His Book," lines 127–28.

and yet we do it imperfectly, often. A very great share of our theological questions, or disputes, originate in the incapacity of the parties to separate truths from their forms, or to see how the same essential truth may clothe itself under forms that are repugnant. There wants to be a large digestion, so to speak, of form in the teacher of theology or mental philosophy, that he may always be aware how the mind and truth, obliged to clothe themselves under the laws of space and sensation, are taking, continually, new shapes or dresses—coming forth poetically, mystically, allegorically, dialectically, fluxing through definitions, symbols, changes of subject and object, yet remaining still the same; for if he is wanting in this, if he is a mere logician, fastening on a word as the sole expression and exact equivalent of a truth, to go on spinning his deductions out of the form of the word, (which yet have nothing to do with the idea,) then he becomes an opinionist only, quarreling, as for truth itself, with all who chance to go out of his word; and, since words are given, not to imprison souls, but to express them, the variations continually indulged by others are sure to render him as miserable in his anxieties, as he is meagre in his contents, and busy in his quarrels. . . .

9. Since all words, but such as relate to necessary truths, are inexact representations of thought, mere types or analogies, or, where the types are lost beyond recovery, only proximate expressions of the thoughts named; it follows that language will be ever trying to mend its own deficiencies, by multiplying its forms of representation. As, too, the words made use of generally carry something false with them, as well as something true, associating form with the truths represented, when really there is no form; it will also be necessary, on this account, to multiply words or figures, and thus to present the subject on opposite sides or many sides. Thus, as form battles form, and one form neutralizes another, all the insufficiencies of words are filled out, the contrarieties liquidated, and the mind settles into a full and just apprehension of the pure spiritual truth. Accordingly we never come so near to a truly well rounded view of any truth, as when it is offered paradoxically; that is, under contradictions; that is, under two or more dictions, which, taken as dictions, are contrary one to the other.

Hence the marvelous vivacity and power of that famous representation of Pascal: "What a chimera, then, is man! What a novelty! What a chaos! What a subject of contradiction! A judge of every thing, and yet a feeble worm of the earth; the depository of truth, and yet a mere heap of uncertainty; the glory and the outcast of the universe. If he boasts, I humble him; if he humbles himself, I boast of him; and always contradict him, till he is brought to comprehend that he is an incomprehensible monster."*

* [Ed.] See Blaise Pascal, *Pensees*, fragment 131 (Lafuma edition).

Scarcely inferior in vivacity and power is the familiar passage of Paul;—"as deceivers, and yet true; as unknown, and yet well known; as dying, and behold, we live; as chastened, and not killed; as sorrowful, yet always rejoicing; as poor, yet making many rich; as having nothing, yet possessing all things."*

So, also, it will be found, that the poets often express their most inexpressible, or evanescent thoughts, by means of repugnant or somewhat paradoxical epithets; as, for example, Coleridge, when he says,—

"The stilly murmer of the distant sea
Tells us of silence."†

Precisely here, too, I suppose, we come upon what is really the true conception of the Incarnation and the Trinity. These great Christian mysteries or paradoxes, come to pass under the same conditions or laws which pertain to langauge. All words are, in fact, only incarnations, or insensings of thought. If we investigate the relations of their forms to the truths signified, we have the same mystery before us; if we set the different, but related forms in comparison, we have the same aspect of repugnance or inconsistency. And then we have only to use the repugnant forms as vehicles of pure thought, dismissing the contradictory matter of the forms, and both words and the Word are understood without distraction,—all by the same process.

Probably, the most contradictory book in the world is the Gospel of John; and that, for the very reason that it contains more and loftier truths than any other. No good writer, who is occupied in simply expressing truth, is ever afraid of inconsistencies or self-contradictions in his language. It is nothing to him that a quirk of logic can bring him into absurdity. If at any time he offers definitions, it is not to get a footing for the play of his logic, but it is simply as multiplying forms or figures of that which he seeks to communicate—just as one will take his friend to different points of a landscape, and show him cross views, in order that he may get a perfect conception of the outline. Having nothing but words in which to give definitions, he understands the impossibility of definitions as determinate measures of thought, and gives them only as being *other forms* of the truth in question, by aid of which it may be more adequately conceived. On the other hand, a writer without either truth or genius, a mere prosaic and literal wordsman, is just the man to magnify definitions. He has never a doubt of their possibility. He lays them down as absolute measures, then draws along his deductions, with cautious consistency, and works out, thus, what he considers to be the exact infallible truth. But his definitions will be found to hang, of necessity, on some

---

* [Ed.] II Corinthians 6:8–10.
† [Ed.]Samuel Taylor Coleridge, "The Eolian Harp," lines 11–12.

word or symbol, that symbol to have drawn every thing to itself, or into its own form, and then, when his work is done, it will be both consistent and false,—false, because of its consistency.

10. It is part of the same view, that logic itself is a defective, and often deceitful instrument. I speak not here of logic as a science, but of that deductive, proving, spinning method of practical investigation, commonly denoted by the term *logical*. It is very obvious, that no turn of logical deduction can prove anything, by itself, not previously known by inspection or insight. And yet, there is always a busy-minded class of sophists or speculators, who, having neither a large observation, nor a power of poetic insight, occupy themselves as workers in words and propositions, managing to persuade themselves and others that they are great investigators, and even discoverers of truth. . . .

It seems to be supposed, or rather assumed, by the class of investigators commonly called logical, that after the subject matter of truth has been gotten into propositions, and cleared, perhaps, by definitions, the faculty of intuition, or insight, may be suspended, and we may go on safely, to reason upon the forms of the words themselves, or the "analogy the words bear to each other." And so, by the mere handling of words and propositions, they undertake to evolve, or, as they commonly speak, to *prove* important truths. They reason, not by or through formulas, but upon them. After the formulas are got ready, they shut their eyes to all interior inspection of their terms, as in algebra, and commit themselves to the mere grammatic laws or predications of their words—expecting, under these, by inversion, evolution, equation, *reductio ad absurdum*, and the like, to work out important results. And this is popularly called *reasoning*. . . .

But suppose the algebraist had no fixed quantities out of which to make his formulas; that his terms were only tropes for certain ideas that have no definite measure, affirming, of course, something not true, as well as something true; suppose that definitions were impossible, save that one trope may sometimes help out another, and that paradoxes are quite as often needed to help out the infirmity, or displace the one-sidedness of definitions. Suppose that all his connective signs, his equations, his evolutions of formula, were indeterminate, and his process never true, save in a certain analogical and poetic sense—what figure, in such a case, would he make with his algebraic process? A glance in this direction suffices to show that the only real and true reasoning, on moral subjects, is that which never embarks on words and propositions, but which holds a constant insight of all terms and constructions—"diligently examining the analogy or relation betwixt words and things. . . ."*

* [Ed.] For the historical context of Bushnell's views on the contrast between "logical"

It will . . . be observed, that our mere reasoners and provers in words, in order to get their formulas arrayed for action, always rule out, or clear away, those antagonistic figures, paradoxes, and contrarious representations, by means of which only a full and comprehensive expression of the truth is possible. They are great in the detection of disagreements, or what they call contradictions; and the finding out of such elements, or the reducing of another to this bad dilemma, by their constructive process, they suppose to be a real triumph of intelligence—which is the same as to say that they can endure none but a one-sided view of truth.

It will almost always happen, also, to this class of investigators, that, when reasoning of man, life, self-active being, God, and religion, they will take up their formulas under the conditions of cause and effect, or space and time, or set them under the atomic relations or inorganic matter. Discussing the human will, for example, or the great question of liberty, the writer will be overpowered by the terms and predicates of language; which being mostly derived from the physical world, are charged, to the same extent, with a mechanical significance. And then we shall have a sophism, great or small, according to his capacity—a ponderous volume, it may be, of formulas, filled up, rolled about, inverted, crossed and twisted—a grand, stupendous, convoluted sophism—all a mere outward practice, however, on words and propositions, in which, as they contain a form of cause and effect in their own nature, it is easily made out that human liberty is the liberty of a scale-beam, turned by the heavier weights. Meantime, the question is only a question of consciousness, one in which the simple decision of consciousness is final;—to which, argument, whether good or bad, can really add nothing, from which nothing take.*

As great mischief and perplexity is often wrought by raising the question of before and after, under the laws of time. The speculative, would-be philosopher wants to be able always to say which is first in the soul's action—this or that. What endless debates have we had in theology concerning questions of priority—whether faith is before repentance, or repentance before faith; whether one or the other is before love, or love before them both; whether justification is before sanctification, and the like. We seem to suppose that a soul can be taken to pieces, or have its exercises parted and put under laws of time, so that we can see them go, in regular clock-work order. Whereas, being *alive* in God when it is truly

and "analogical" or figurative thinking, see Donald Crosby, *Horace Bushnell's Theory of Language* (The Hague: Mouton, 1975), pp. 79–120.

* [Ed.] Bushnell associates this "scale-beam" analogy with Jonathan Edwards' treatment of human choice in *The Freedom of the Will*. For a similar, more complete critique of Edwards and the "New England Theology" generally on this point, see Bushnell, *Nature and the Supernatural* (New York: Charles Scribner, 1858), pp. 46–54.

united to Him, its right exercises, being functions of life, are of course mutual conditions one of another. Passing out of mechanism, or the empire of dead atoms, into the plastic realm of life, all questions of before and after we leave behind us. We do not ask whether the heart causes the heaving of the lungs, or whether the lungs have priority, and keep up the beating of the heart; or whether the digestive faculty is first in time, or the assimilative, or the nervous. We look at the whole body as a vital nature, and finding every function alive, every fibre active, we perceive that all the parts, even the minutest, exist and act as mutual conditions one of another. And so it is in spiritual life. Every grace supposes every other as its condition, and time is wholly out of the question. But, the moment any one of our atomizing and mechanising speculators comes into the field, the question of priority is immediately raised. Perceiving that love seems to imply or involve faith, he declares that faith is first. Then, as another is equally sure that faith implies love, he maintains that love is first. A third, in the same way, that repentance is before both; a fourth, that both are before repentance. And now we have a general debate on hand, in which the formulas will be heard ringing as flails, for a dozen years, or a century. Meantime, it will happen that all the several schools of wisdom are at fault, inasmuch as none of the priorities are first, or rather all are first; being all conditions mutually of one another. Might it not have been better, at the first, to clear ourselves of time and the law it weaves into words and predicates—to perceive, as by a little insight we may, that, in all vital and plastic natures, the functions have a mutual play?. . .

12. What Goethe says of himself is true of all efficient writers:—"I have always regarded all I have done, as solely symbolical, and, at bottom, it does not signify whether I make pots or dishes." And then, what Eckerman says of him in his preface, follows of course. "Goethe's detached remarks upon poetry, have often an appearance of contradiction. Sometimes he lays all the stress on the material which the outward world affords, sometimes upon that which is given to the inward world of the poet; sometimes the greatest importance is attached to the subject, sometimes to the mode of treating it; sometimes all is made to depend on perfection of form, sometimes form is to be neglected, and all the attention paid to the spirit. But all these seeming contradictions are, in fact, only successive presentations of single sides of a truth, which, by their union, manifest completely to us its existence, and guide us to a perception of its nature. I confide in the insight and comprehensive power of the cultivated reader, not to stop at any one part, as seen by itself, but to keep his eye on the significance of the whole, and by that

means, to bring each particular truth into its proper place and relations."*

Is it a fault of Goethe that he must be handled in this manner? Rather is it one of the highest proofs of his genius and the real greatness of his mind. Had he been willing to stay under some one figure, and draw himself out into formal consistency, throwing off none of these bold antagonisms, he must have been a very different character—not Goethe, but some dull proser or male spinster of logic, never heard of by us.

What, then, shall we say of Christ and the Gospel of John? If it requires such an array of antagonisms to set forth the true idea of poetry, what does it require to set forth God and redemption? What should we expect, in such a work, but a vast compilation of symbols and of forms, which to the mere wordsman, are contrary to each other? And then what shall we do?—what, for example, with the trinity, the atonement, the bondage and freedom of sin? Shall we say, with the infidel, this is all a medley of contradiction—mere nonsense, fit only to be rejected? Shall we take up these bold antagonisms, as many orthodox believers have done, seize upon some one symbol as the real form of the truth, and compel all the others to submit to it; making, thus as may sects as there are symbols, and as many petty wars about each truth as it has sides or inches of surface? Or shall we endeavor, with the Unitarians, to decoct the whole mass of symbol, and draw off the extract into pitchers of our own; fine, consistent, nicely-rounded pitchers, which, so far from setting out any where towards infinity, we can carry at pleasure by the handle, and definitely measure by the eye? What critic has even thought of handling Goethe in the methods just named? We neither scout his inconsistency, nor drill him into some one of his forms, nor decoct him into forms of our own. But we call him the many-sided great man; we let him stand in his own chosen symbols, whether they be "pots or dishes," and do him the greater honor because of the complexity and the magnificent profusion of his creations.

There is no book in the world that contains so many repugnances, or antagonistic forms of assertion, as the Bible. Therefore, if any man please to play off his constructive logic upon it, he can easily show it up as the absurdest book in the world. But whosoever wants, on the other hand, really to behold and receive all truth, and would have the truth-world overhang him as an empyrean of stars, complex, multitudinous, striving antagonistically, yet comprehended, height above height, and deep under deep, in a boundless score of harmony; what man soever,

---

* [Ed.] Bushnell's source for this passage is Margaret Fuller's translation of Eckermann's *Conversatons with Goethe* (Boston: Hillard, Gray, and Company, 1829), p. 6. It is worth noting that Fuller's translation was commissioned by Geoge Ripley for his series, Specimens of Foreign Standard Literature—a thoroughly Transcendental affair!

content with no small rote of logic and catechism, reaches with true
hunger after this, and will offer himself to the many-sided forms of the
scripture with a perfectly ingenuous and receptive spirit; he shall find his
nature flooded with senses, vastnesses, and powers of truth, such as it is
even greatness to feel. God's own lawgivers, heroes, poets, historians,
prophets, and preachers and doers of righteousness, will bring him their
company, and representing each his own age, character, and mode of
thought, shine upon him as so many cross lights on his field of knowledge, to give him the most complete and manifold view possible of
every truth. He has not only the words of Christ, the most manifold of
all teachers, but he has gospels which present him in his different words
and attitudes; and then, besides, he has four, some say five, distinct writers of epistles, who follow, giving each his own view of the doctrine of
salvation and the Christian life, (views so unlike or antagonistical that
many have regarded them as being quite irreconcilable)—Paul, the dialectic, commonly so called; John, the mystic; James, the moralizer; Peter,
the homilectic; and perhaps a fifth in the epistle to the Hebrews, who is
a Christian templar and Hebraizer. The Old Testament corresponds.
Never was there a book uniting so many contrarious aspects of one and
the same truth. The more complete, therefore, because of its manifold-
ness; nay, the more really harmonious, for its apparent want of harmony.

How, then, are we to receive it and come into its truth? Only in the
comprehensive manner just now suggested; not by destroying the repugnances, but by allowing them to stand, offering our mind to their
impressions, and allowing it to gravitate inwardly, towards that whole of
truth, in which they coalesce. And when we are in that whole, we shall
have no dozen propositions of our own in which to give it forth; neither
will it be a whole which we can set before the world, standing on one
leg, in a perfectly definite shape, clear of all mystery: but it will be such
a whole as requires a whole universe of rite, symbol, incarnation, historic
breathings, and poetic fires, to give it expression—in a word, just what it
now has. Finding it not a Goethe, but as much greater than he as God is
greater than a genius of our own human race, when we think of ourselves trying to give out the substantial import of the volume in a few
scant formulas, it will probably occur to us just to ask what figure we
should make, in a similar attempt upon one who is no more than a German poet? And then, it will not be strange if we drop our feeble, blood-
less sentences and dogmas, whether of belief or denial, and return, duly
mortified, into the faith of those august and magnificent forms of scripture—incarnation; Father, Son and Holy Ghost; atonement as blood, life,
sacrifice, propitiation, ransom, liberty, regeneration, wisdom, righteousness, sanctification, and redemption—the great mystery of godliness.

13. The views of language and interpretation I have here offered,

suggest the very great difficulty, if not impossibility of mental science and religious dogmatism. In all such uses or attempted uses, the effort is to make language answer a purpose that is against its nature. The "winged words" are required to serve as beasts of burden; or, what is no better, to forget their poetic life, as messengers of the air, and stand still, fixed upon the ground, as wooden statues of truths. Which, if they seem to do; if, to comfort our studies of dogma, they assume the inert faces we desire, and suffer us to arrange the fixed attitudes of their bodies, yet, as little Memnons touched and made vocal by the light, they will be discoursing still of the free empyrean, disturbing, and scattering, by their voices, all the exact meanings we had thought to hold them to, in the nice corporeal order of our science.

In algebra and geometry, the ideas themselves being absolute, the terms or names also may be; but in mental science and religion, no such exactness is possible, because our apprehensions of truth are here only proximate and relative. I see not, therefore, how the subject matter of mental science and religion can ever be included under the fixed forms of dogma. Definitions cannot bring us over the difficulty; for definitions are, in fact, only changes of symbol, and, if we take them to be more, will infallibly lead us into error. In fact, no man is more certain to run himself into mischievous error, than he who places implicit confidence in definitions. After all, definitions will be words, and science will be words, and words, place them in whatever shapes we may, will be only shadows of truth.

Accordingly, it will ever be found, that in mental science, the investigators are, in fact, only trying to see if they can make up a true man out of some ten or twenty or forty words in the dictionary. The phrenologists claim to have done it, and even to show us the localities of these words in our heads, and how very man-like their word-elements will work when put together. All the systems are plausible—some, we are told, are infallible—the last and completed results of mental science! And yet there seem to be questions coming after. And probably it will be found, after all, that the only way to make up a real man is to put the whole dictionary into him; and then, most likely, some spaces will be found vacant, some members wanting. It will also be required, too, that the words be not packed together mechanically in the man, but that they all be alive in him—one living, plastic, organically perfect whole—acting, however, a little mysteriously sometimes, as the life-power even of an egg or a bean will presume to do; or what is more confusive to theory, acting diseasedly and contrarily, as if life had let in death, and a quarrel for possession were going on within. And then, if our complete dictionary man should be finally produced, alive, mysterious, acting diseasedly, in what shape would the now completed science be as likely to emerge, as in those forms of life which a Shakespeare, or some great

universal poet of humanity might set before us? Poets, then, are the true
metaphysicians, and if there be any complete science of man to come,
they must bring it.

Is it to be otherwise in religion? Can there be produced, in human
language, a complete and proper Christian theology; can the Christian
truth be offered in the molds of any dogmatic statement? What is the
Christian truth? Pre-eminently and principally, it is the expression of
God—God coming into expression, through histories and rites, through an
incarnation, and through language—in one syllable, by the WORD. The
endeavor is, by means of expression, and under the laws of expression, to
set forth God—His providence, and His government, and, what is more
and higher than all, God's own feeling, His truth, love, justice, compassion.
Well, if it be something for a poet to express man, it is doubtless somewhat
more for a book to be constructed that will express God, and open His
eternity to man. And if it would be somewhat difficult to put the poet of
humanity into a few short formulas, that will communicate all he
expresses, with his manifold, wondrous art, will it probably be easier to
transfer the grand poem of salvation, that which expresses God, even the
feeling of God, into a few dull propositions; which, when they are produced, we may call the sum total of the Christian truth? Let me freely
confess that, when I see the human teacher elaborating a phrase of speech,
or mere dialectic proposition, that is going to tell what God could only
show me by the history of ages, and the mystic life and death of Jesus our
Lord, I should be deeply shocked by his irreverence, if I were not rather
occupied with pity for his infirmity.

It ought not to be necessary to remind any reader of the bible, that
religion has a natural and profound alliance with poetry. Hence, a very
large share of the bible is composed of poetic contributions. Another
share, equally large, is that which comes to us in a form of history and
fact; that is, of actual life, which is equally remote from all abstractions,
and, in one view, equally poetic; for history is nothing but an evolution
or expression of God and man in their own nature and character. The
teachings of Christ are mere utterances of truth, not argumentations over
it. He gives it forth in living symbols, without definition, without *proving* it, ever, as the logicians speak, well understanding that truth is that
which shines in its own evidence, that which *finds* us, to use an admira-
ble expression of Coleridge, and thus enters into us. . . .

We find little, therefore, in the scriptures, to encourage the hope of a
complete and sufficient Christian dogmatism, or of a satisfactory and truly
adequate system of scientific theology. Language, under the laws of logic
or speculation, does not seem to be adequate to any such use or purpose.
The scriptures of God, in providing a clothing for religious truth, have little
to do with mere dialectics, much to do with the freer creations of poetry;
and that for reasons, evidently, which ought to waken a salutary scepticism

in us, in regard to the possibility of that, which so many great minds have been attempting with so great confidence for so many hundreds of years. With due respect, also, I will venture to ask, whether the actual results of this immense engineering process, which we call dogmatic and polemic theology—as surely polemic as dogmatic—does not give some countenance to the doubt I am suggesting? . . .

It accords, also, with this, that while natural science is advancing with so great rapidity and certainty of movement, the advances of mental science and theology are so irregular and obscure, and are wrought out by a process so conflicting and tortuous. They seem in fact, to have no advance, save what may be called a cultivation of symbol, produced by the multifarious industry of debate and system-making. There is, however, one hope for mental and religious truth, and their final settlement, which I confess I see but dimly, and can but faintly express, or indicate. It is, that physical science, leading the way, setting outward things in their true proportions, opening up their true contents, revealing their genesis and final causes and laws, and weaving all into the unity of a real universe, will so perfect our knowledges and conceptions of them, that we can use them, in the second department of language, with more exactness. There is, we have also seen, in what we call nature, that is, in its objects, an outward grammar of relations, which constructs the grammar of language; or what is not far different, the logic of propositions. In the laws of nature, I suppose, there is, in like manner, an internal grammar, which is certain, as it is evolved, to pass into language, and be an internal grammar in that, systematizing and steadying its uses. And then language will be as much more full and intelligent, as it has more of God's intelligence, in the system of nature, imparted to its symbols. For, undoubtedly, the whole universe of nature is a perfect analogon of the whole universe of thought or spirit. Therefore, as nature becomes truly a universe only through science revealing its universal laws, the true universe of thought and spirit cannot sooner be conceived. It would be easy to show, in this connection, the immense force already exerted over the empire of spiritual truth by astronomy, chemistry, geology, the revelations of light and electricity, and especially of the mysterious and plastic workings of life, in the animal and vegetable kingdoms. We are accustomed to say, that this is not the same world to live in that it was fifty years ago. Just as true is it, that it is not the same world to *think* in, that it then was,—of which, also, we shall, by and by, take notice.

If, then, it please any one to believe, notwithstanding the present incapacities of dogmatism, that when, through science, we are able to see things physical in their true force and relations, having, also, within us, inbreathed by the spirit of God, a comprehensive heart and feelings sufficiently cleared of prejudice, to behold, in the universal mirror of God, His universal truth,—if, I say, any one please to believe, that now the Christian world may arrive at some final and determinate apprehensions of Christian doctrine, I will not object. But, if they do, observe, it will only be that they have settled, at last, into a comprehensive reception of the universal symbolism, and not that they have invented a few propositions, so intensely significant and true, as to dispense with all besides.

14. It is important to notice, as connected with the subject of language, that dogmatical propositions, such as are commonly woven into creeds and catechisms of doctrine, have not the certainty they are commonly supposed to have. They only give us the seeing of the authors, at the precise stand-point occupied by them, at the time, and they are true only as seen from that point,—not even there, save in a proximate sense. Passing on, descending the current of time, we will say, for two centuries, we are brought to a different point, as when we change positions in a landscape, and then we are doomed to see things in a different light, in spite of ourselves. It is not that the truth changes, but that we change. Our eye changes color, and then the color of our eye affects our seeing. We are different men, living as parts in a different system of things and thinkings, denyings, and affirmings; and, as our contents and our antagonisms are different, we cannot see the same truths in the same forms. It may even be necessary to change the forms, to hold us in the same truths.

I could name phrases that have been brought into the creeds of many of our New England churches, within the present half century, which are already waxing old, and are doomed, within the next half century, to ask a re-modification.

Besides, in the original formation of any creed, catechism, or system of divinity, there is always a latent element of figure, which, probably, the authors know not of, but without which, it is neither true to them, nor to anybody. But in a long course of repetition, the figure dies out, and the formula settles into a literality, and then, if the repetition goes on, it is really an assent to what is not true; for that which was true, at the beginning, has now become untrue—and that, however paradoxical it may seem, by being assented to. What I here speak of, might be easily illustrated by a reference to the dogmatic history of opinions, concerning sin and free will. The will is under no mechanical laws. Hence, in all the reasonings, affirmations, and denials relating to the will and its modes of responsible activity, language, being mostly derived from the mechanical world, must somehow be divorced, in the use, from all its mechanical laws, else it imports a falsity. But the difficulty is, to keep the language up to that self-active unmechanical sense in which, only, it was true in the original use; for a dull, unthinking repetition lets it down very soon under the old mechanical laws, and then the same, or closely similar, forms of reasoning and assertion are false. Hence, in part, the necessity, I suppose, that this particular class of subjects should be reinvestigated every fifty years. Considering the infirmities of language, therefore, all formulas of doctrine should be held in a certain spirit of accommodation. They cannot be pressed to the letter, for the very sufficient reason that the letter is never true. They can be regarded only as proximate representations, and should therefore be accepted not as laws over belief, or opinion, but more as badges of consent and good understanding. The moment we begin to speak of them as guards and tests of purity, we confess that we have lost the sense of purity, and, with about equal certainty, the virtue itself.

At the same time, it is remarkable with what ease a man, who is sensible of the fluxing nature and significance of words, may assent to almost any creed, and that, with a perfectly sincere doubt, whether he does not receive it in its most interior and real meaning; that is, whether going back to the men who made it, taking their stand point, and abating what belongs to the form of a truth, in distinction from the truth itself, he does not come into the real senses or interior beliefs they clothed in these forms. Perhaps it is on this account that I have never been able to sympathize, at all, with the abundant protesting of the New England Unitarians, against creeds. So far from suffering even the least consciousness of constraint, or oppression, under any creed, I have been readier to accept as great a number as fell in my way; for when they are subjected to the deepest chemistry of thought, that which descends to the point of relationship between the form of the truth and its interior formless nature, they become, thereupon, so elastic, and run so freely into each other, that one seldom need have any difficulty in accepting as many as are offered him. He may regard them as only a kind of battle-dooring or words, blow answering to blow, while the reality of the play, viz. *exercise*, is the same, whichever side of the room is taken, and whether the stroke is given by the right hand or the left. . . .

15. [I]t is the right of every author, who deserves attention at all, to claim a certain liberty, and even to have it for a merit that he cannot be judged exactly by old uses and formulas. Life is organic; and if there be life in his work, it will be found not in some noun or verb that he uses, but in the organic whole of his creations. Hence, it is clear that he must be apprehended in some sense, as a whole, before his full import can be received in paragraphs and sentences. Until then, he will, of necessity, appear to be obscure, enigmatical, extravagant, or even absurd. He cannot be tested by the jingle of his words, or by auscultation applied to the breathing of his sentences. No decree of condemnation must be passed upon him, because he does not make himself understood, sentence by sentence; for if he infuses into words a life-power of his own, or does

more than simply to recombine old impressions, he cannot make himself intelligible, fully, save through a kind of general acquaintance. It may, even, be to his praise, that he is not too easily understood. For, in this matter of understanding, two things are requisite; first, a matter which is understandable; and, second, a power that is capable of understanding; and if there be some things offered, hard to be understood, then there must be a power of digestion strong enough to master them; and if, in fault of that, some crude, and over-confident sophister dangerously wrests the words, the blame is with him. Nor is it enough, in such a case, that the reading man, or public, be of a naturally sound mind, or even that they bring to the subject, capacities of a very high order; for words, as we have seen, never carry, or transfer a thought; they only offer hints or symbols, to put others on generating the same thought, which, in many cases, they are not likely to do, unless they have been long enough practiced in the subject discussed, to know where it lies; and not even then, if the writer is at all out of the system of his day, without such a degree of exercise in his forms of thought as will beget a certain general insight of his method and symbol.

They cannot run to a dictionary, and draw out the shroud of an old meaning from that, by which to conceive, or in which to clothe words and phrases that have their vital force, in no small part, from the man himself; and which, therefore, can be fully understood only by reference to the total organism of which they are members. The reading man, therefore, before he thinks to judge the writing man, must first endeavor to generate the writing man. And this, without supposing any defect of capacity in himself, will sometimes be difficult. He may be too young, or too old; having too little breadth, or too little flexibility, to make a sufficient realization of the truth presented. It costs me no mortification, to confess that the most fructifying writer I ever read, was one in whom I was, at first, able only to see glimpses, or gleams of truth; one whom it required years of study and reflection, of patient suspension and laborious self-questioning, to be able fully to understand; and, indeed, whom I never since have read, at all, save in a chapter or two, which I glanced over, just to see how obvious and clear, what before was impossible, had now become.*

Shall I dare to go further? Shall I say that of all the "clear" writers and speakers I have ever met with,—those, I mean, who are praised by the multitude for their transparency,—I have never yet found one that was able to send me forward an inch; or one that was really true, save in

---

* [Ed.] Bushnell probably has Coleridge in mind here. See a very similar statement on his relation to Coleridge's works quoted in Mary Bushnell Cheney, *The Life and Letters of Horace Bushnell* (New York: Harper and Brothers, 1880; rpt. New York: Arno Press, Inc., 1969), pp. 207–8.

a certain superficial, or pedagogical sense, as being an accurate distributor of that which is known. The roots of the known are always in the unknown, and, if a man will never show the root of any thing, if he will treat of the known as *separate* from the unknown, and as having a complete knowledge of it, which he has not—pretending, still, to be an investigator, and to exert an obstetric force, when he is only handling over old knowledges and impressions—he may easily enough be clear. Nothing, in fact, is easier, if one is either able to be shallow, or willing to be false. He is clear, because he stands out *before* the infinite and the unknown; separated, bounded off [de-finite] so that you see the whole compass of his head, just so many inches in diameter. But the writer, who is to help us on, by some real advance or higher revelation, will, for that reason, be less comprehensible, and offer more things hard to be understood. He will be, as it were, a face, setting *out from* a background of mystery; a symbolism, through which the infinite and the unknown are looking out upon us, and by kind significances, tempting us to struggle into that holy, but dark profound, which they are opening. Of course, we are not to make a merit of obscurity; for nothing is more to be admired than the wondrous art by which some men are able to propitiate and assist the generative understanding of others, so as to draw them readily into higher realizations of truth. But there is a limit, we must acknowledge, even to this highest power of genius; it cannot quite create a soul under the ribs of death.

Whatever may be thought of these suggestions, for some, I suppose, will give them little weight, it is obvious that, since language is rather an instrument of suggestion, than of absolute conveyance for thought, since it acts suggestively, through symbols held up in the words, which symbols and words are never exact measures of any truth (always imputing somewhat of form to the truth which does not belong to it, always somewhat contrary to each other)—this being true, it is obvious that a very little of perverse effort expended on his words, can subject a writer to almost any degree of apparent absurdity. And, what is specially to be noticed, there is no other human work, in which so much of applause can be gotten at so cheap a rate, and with so small a modicum of talent. The work, indeed, is always half done beforehand. The words are ready to quarrel, as soon as any one will see them, and nothing is necessary, in fact, but to play off a little of constructive ingenuity on their forms, to set them at war with one another and the whole universe besides. And, when it is done, many will be sure to admire and praise what they call the profound and searching logic displayed. Now, the truth is, that no many-sided writer, no one who embraces all the complementary forces of truth, is ever able to stand in harmony before himself, (such is the nature of language,) save by an act of internal construction favorable to himself, and preservative of his mental unity. It follows, of necessity, that without this favorable act of construction extended to his words, no true teacher can be saved from contradiction and confusion,—no one, especially, who presents more than a half, or tenth part of a truth. Therefore, every writer, not manifestly actuated by a malignant or evil spirit, is entitled to this indulgence. The mind must be offered up to him, for the time, with a certain degree of sympathy. It must draw itself into the same position; take his constructions; feel out, so to speak, his meanings, and keep him, as far as may be, in a form of general consistency. Then, having endeavored thus, and for a sufficient length of time, to reproduce him or his thought, that is, to make a realization of him, some proper judgment may be formed in regard to the soundness of his doctrine. . . .

It needs also to be remarked, in this connection, that a writer is not, of course, to be blamed because he is variously interpreted by his readers, or because the public masses have a degree of difficulty in conceiving his precise meaning. It should be so, and will be, if he has any thing of real moment to say. There has always been most of controversy, for this reason, about the meaning of the greatest authors and teachers,—Plato, for example, and Aristotle; Bacon, Shakespeare, and Goethe; Job, Paul, John, and especially CHRIST HIMSELF. What, in fact, do we see, in the endless debate, kept up for these eighteen hundred years, over the words of Jesus, but an illustration of the truth, that infinitesimals, though there be many of them, are not the best judges of infinites. And something of the same principle pertains, in the judgment or inspection of merely human teachers. They may be obscure, not from weakness only, which, certainly, is most frequent, but quite as truly by reason of their exceeding breadth, and the piercing vigor of their insight. And when this latter is true, as it sometimes may be, then to invoke a sentence of popular condemnation, because the writer has not made himself perfectly intelligible, or clear to the whole public, is, in fact, to assist or instigate the multitude in practicing a fraud against themselves. And, what is worse, if possible, it encourages an ill-natured and really unchristian spirit in them, excusing their impatience with every form of teaching that requires an effort of candor, or an ingenuous spirit.

## From *Christ in Theology*,
## "Language and Doctrine" (1851)*

A single principle, distinctly apprehended and carefully traced, will be found to comprise all that is peculiar in the views presented in my book.† In this principle you have a key to my real meaning, and without this principle constantly held in mind, and applied as a key, my language will only lead you into impressions which are totally remote from my real sentiments. The principle is this:

THAT ALL RELIGIOUS TRUTH, AS WELL THEOLOGICAL AS PRACTICAL, IS AND MUST BE PRESENTED UNDER CONDITIONS OF FORM OR ANALOGY FROM THE OUTWARD STATE.

The truth-feeling power of the soul may have truth present immediately to it, or may directly intuit truth, without symbols or representations of language. But the moment it will think discursively, or represent to another any subject of thought, that subject must be clothed in forms that are only signs or analogies, and not equivalents of the truth. Even definitions and the most abstract modes of terminology will be true only in a sense more or less visibly formal and analogical. They will carry their sense, not by simple notation, as in arithmetic or algebra, but as offering it to the critical power of the eye and heart in symbols naturally expressive.

Assuming, or having established this position concerning language, the person of Christ, the trinity, the atonement, and other great truths of revelation, must be taken as offered to us under the conditions and laws of expression or simple presentation, as a soul is expressed or presented in a face, and not as in the formula of a merely logical calculus,—interpreted and not overlaid by constructive judgments. My conviction is, that all our difficulties and controversies, in respect to these great truths of revelation, are caused by a misuse of the material offered us. The truth is given us in forms or images naturally expressive; we take these forms to be the very truths themselves, and immediately begin to reason upon them by constructive, or by what are sometimes called,

* [Ed.] *Christ in Theology* (Hartford: Brown and Parsons, 1851), pp. 15–89. Included here: pp. 15–18, 31–34, 64–67, 79–84, 86–87.

† [Ed.] Bushnell is referring to *God in Christ*, to which *Christ in Theology* is a polemical sequel.

though improperly, a priori judgments. They are a priori in pretense or appearance, but in fact are only mock uses of this method of reasoning, having no basis in the real truth of the premise, but only a plausible show of reason in the *form* of the premise.

This, I conceive, is the almost universal sin that infests the reasonings of mankind concerning moral and spiritual subjects, and it is this at which I aimed in the deprecations of logic, or the logical method, that are offered here and there in my book. It was not my design to make an assault upon logic itself as a science. I was not ignorant that all the sublime results of the calculus are fruits of genuine logic. I only meant that, as soon as we carry this method into moral and religious philosophy, and subject our mind to it as a dominant influence there, we are sure to be enveloped in sophistries without end or limit; for words, in this case, have a wholly different relation to their truths—a relation of form or symbol, and not of mere notation. We must hold them in the way of inspection; we must read them by looking in their faces, as we do our friends. We can not take them into our logical understanding and use them as the terms of a calculus. What they carry into our soul's feeling or perception, or awaken in it by expression, is their only truth, and that is a simple internal state of the soul itself; which if we undertake to handle in any merely logical and a priori method, we are sure to abuse both ourselves and it. And it is by just this abuse of Scripture, reasoning out of its forms, and supposing that we reason out of the truth itself, that theology is made to wear a look of confusion so unrespectable. The free symbols of expression clash, as symbols, with each other, and then we take them as so many centers of logical systems, piling up, age upon age, our Babels of wisdom, confounding worse and worse the language of the skies, till the power of mutual understanding, and even the sense of community in the *truth*, appear to be lost.

Let me illustrate what is intended in these suggestions by a few examples. See how the Romish church establishes one of her infallible world-renowned dogmas. "Is not Jesus," she asks, "God?" "Yes, certainly." "Is not Mary the mother of Jesus?" "Yes." "What, then, is Mary but the Mother of God?—AVE MARIA! Be it henceforth a doctrine of the church, publish it, require it of all people to worship Mary the Mother of God!" Now, in just this manner, a great part of the scholastic theology, nay, of all theology, down to Liberal Christianity itself, is created. By the same false method, we are continually trying all the great questions that pertain to God's being and the work of human salvation.

Do you ask why false,—where is the fault of the argument? There is no fault in the argument, I answer, regarding simply the logic of it. The premises are true, and who will say that the result does not follow? It only happens that the premises are not true, save in a sense so far qualified as to take away the conclusion. Mary is not the mother of Jesus in the same sense that the word *mother* has in its ordinary use. She is only the visible instrument of a Transcendent Power, who is employing her as the medium by which He will graft into human history what is *not* of it, and will be really grafted into it only so far as to answer certain purposes of expression. Neither is Jesus God in any such sense that the name *Jesus* measures God; he is the Word made flesh. His person is representatively God, and not God in the inclusive logical sense that he is the All of God. And so the infallible conclusion, that Mary is the Mother of God, vanishes, the moment we look into the simple truth of expression that lies in the premises. . . .

Perhaps it is *one of the highest errands of our life to learn the method of finding truths in their forms*; to learn how easy it is, by a false use of words, to fill our minds with the most contradictory and mischievous errors; to be practiced and established in the simple and delicately ingenuous use that reads all truths in the faces and signs of things that reveal them. Possibly this will be the crowning distinction of heavenly minds, that they are able to read God's eternal language without mistake or hindrance; for I can not but suspect that there is an eternal and necessary connection between the *forms* God has wrought into things,—thus into language,—and the contents, on the one hand, of his own mind, and the principles, on the other, of all created mind. However this may be, would it not be more modest, and far more practical, instead of flying to the heavens to be emancipated from what God has given us here, to return again to our words and our signs, and ask if, possibly, there may not be some better, more legitimate and honest use of them, by which we may know more and pretend less, have more to communicate, and less of strife and judgment?

This certainly has been my conviction. I had no such thought as that I was making light of truth, and reflecting distrust and discouragement on reasonable and proper efforts to find the truth. I supposed, rather, that I was showing how we may open a wider heaven of truth than our own or all mere formulas and abstractions could possibly contain. I supposed that I was showing how a suspension of our intensely dogmatizing habit; how the ceasing to be busied *about* and *upon* truth, as a dead body offered to the scalpels of logic, and the giving ourselves to truth as set before us in living expression, under God's own forms, yielding them a pure heart in which to glass themselves, would fill us evermore with senses of God and his truth otherwise unattainable. I supposed that, if we can but quit our over-theoretic and abstractive wisdom, make a great deal less of the plausible ingenuities of system, be simple enough to think more of receiving and less of constructing, and to offer a living ingenuous heart to what God *expresses* to us, we should be no longer drawn off into petty formulas, to fight for the mere *minima* of truth, arrayed as

METHODIST COLLEGE LIBRARY
Fayetteville, N. C.

086532

in starvation against each other, but should receive so much more of God's fullness, and spread ourselves in such a breadth of comprehension as to find the unity, whose loss we deplore, in simply receiving truths whose loss was unknown—hidden from us, by the party zeal we had for systems that contained only a few small segments or specks of truth.

Language is not an instrument so imperfect, when rightly accepted, or used according to its real nature. If instead of occupying our "dying thoughts," and our conceptions of "another life," with conjectures of some better medium that will deliver us from the obscurity and limitation of this, we could simply turn ourselves to the practical question, by what abuses and perversions we become involved in so great confusion of doctrine, and reduce ourselves to so great poverty in the truth, we should discover that there is truth enough to be known here, and truth enough expressed,—only provided we had eyes to see it. Nay, if there be any advantage to accrue from a change of worlds, we should begin to suspect that it will be found, not so much in better media, as in a more sensible and proper use. The principal difficulty we have with language now is, that it will not put into the theoretic understanding what the imagination only can receive, and will not open to the head what the heart only can interpret. It is a great trouble with us that we can not put a whole scheme of redemption, which God could execute only by the volume of expression contained in the life and death of his incarnate Son, into a theologic formula or article of ten words. It is as if, being unable to compress the whole tragic force of Lear into some one sentence of Edgar's gibberish, we lose our patience, and cry out upon the poverty of language and conception in the poem. Let us only take the attitude of reception; let us cease form our foolish endeavor to make universes of truth for God out of a few words and images that we have speculated into wise sentences; and then turning to his own living forms of expression, brought forth in Scripture and the world and Providence, set ourselves before them as interpreters and learners, with an imagination that is open, and a living and believing heart; we shall then begin to feel that there is abundance of language here, and that, too, which is abundantly significant. If our theology is dull and partial, if we long after a future state where "intuitions" will give us something better than "notions," and "names," and "shadows," we need the transfer after all, not so much to get a new language, as to get away from our own abuse of the language we have. To see God in those things wherein he sets himself before us is the way of intuition, and we need not go to heaven for that; for it is the essential beatitude of "the pure in heart" that "they shall see God" here, as often as they look for Him, and without a change of worlds. . . .

But the question will now be raised, what place have we left for

Christian theology, or for any reliable conception of the Christian scheme of salvation? That I have little respect for pure dogmatism, or for merely speculative theology, is sufficiently apparent; I have not made any secret of the fact. And yet I have a certain conviction, whether I can show the reasons or not, that we must have something, somehow held and exercised, that may be called theology. We must define, distinguish, arrange and frame into order the matter of our knowledge. System is the instinct of intelligence, and to crucify the instinct of system is, in one view, to crucify intelligence. . . .

If all human language is found to be under conditions of form, while truth itself, being spiritual, is out of form, or has no form, it does not follow that Christian doctrine is to be despaired of, or treated with indifference. It is only to be sought with greater patience, a more delicate candor, and a more ingenuous love. And for just this reason, Christian doctrine may be worth a great deal more to the world than it would be, if it could be bolted into the mind by terms of absolute notation, apart from all conditions of candor, justice and sympathy with God or man. If words are insufficient, as I have said, to convey spiritual things in literal senses and exact measures, they are only the more sufficient on that account, when taken as signs offered to candor and the interpreting power of sympathy and spiritual insight. We have words enough, and those which are good enough, if we can use them rightly or according to their true nature. If it requires a degree of sympathy, generously extended and for a length of time, to allow us to come into the whole or sphere of another, and feel out, in that manner, the real import of his words, before we can be sure that we understand him, it ought not to be a hard necessity that a like sympathy with God is requisite to make any true doctrine of God, whether in the words of man or of Scripture, intelligible and clear to the mind; or again that this condition of sympathy requires a large infusion of the Divine Spirit, which is itself a divine experience and an immediate knowledge.

What, though language can tell us nothing true concerning him, save as in forms that need to be interpreted by feeling and can open their light only to a spiritually discerning sympathy; what, though there be in them no real notation for truth, in which, by definitions, equations, inversions and such like operations, we may pile up a scheme of theology or divine knowledge from below, that shall stand and be true, like a treatise in mathematics, simply as being what it is; is it therefore nothing that we can know God as being with us and in us, filling our argumentations, opening to us the senses and powers of words, imparting himself to our secret experience as the light of all seeing, and molding us ever to the state of divine consciousness, which is, at once, the condition and principal substance of knowledge? I certainly think otherwise. Indeed, if it were possible to get religious truth into shapes and formulas having an absolute meaning, like the terms of algebra, as clear even to the wicked as to the pure, and requiring no conditions of character in the receivers, it would very nearly subvert, it seems to me, all that is most significant and sublime in the discipline of life.

The Scriptures, it seems to me, are most divinely wise in the fact that they attempt no such thing, but prefer to offer God and his mystery to the spiritual heart to be spiritually discerned—discerned by love and pure docility and patient experience. They are most perfect as a gift, simply because of what, in one view, may be called their imperfection; that they do not offer God as a market-place currency, in coins of words that coarse and brutish men may handle as knowingly as they who are most like him in spirit; throw him not about upon the ground as pearls to be trodden and champed by the swine of speculative reason; but present him to us glassed in images and forms, to be responsibly interpreted with a delicate reverence and a spirit waiting for the discovery of God. Then he is to be the prize of industry, the reward of purity and love. Then the word is, "ye shall seek me and find me, when ye shall search for me with all your heart."

The student then will be a student, not of theology, but, in the proper sense, of divinity. The knowledge he gets will be divinity, filling his whole consciousness,—a Living State, and not a scheme of wise sentences. He will be a man who understands God as being indoctrinated, or inducted into God, by studies that are themselves inbreathings of the divine love and power. . . .

[So once again] the question returns, what is theology? what place have we for it? what good place can it fill, or good service render?

Of course every right answer to this question will admit that it can not be a law for any thing, not being itself infallible. It is even conceivable that one article of its value consists in the fact that it is not true, or at least not sufficiently true; for every system conceived by man partakes the limitation of man; and yet the system may be wanted to collect his knowledges and frame them into some intelligible order. This will comfort his intelligence. It will give him the method, also, by which to teach what he knows, and learn what he does not. If our generalizations are only General Thumbs, if our systems are only pocket systems of the infinite, they are yet necessary as accommodations to ourselves, and, possibly, are good for what they exclude, as well as for what they contain. They are to the disciple what the iris is to the eye, drawing its opaque and variously-colored curtains round the aperture of sight, that only just so much of the light may enter as will make the tiny picture within distinct and clear.

It is also conceivable, and is probably a serious and momentous truth, that the exercise of system or the endeavor after system, is commonly a greater benefit than the actually resulting systems prepared.

Instigated, in this effort or exercise, by the natural instinct of system, the disciple is made stronger and more competent by his exercise; though he reaches no veritable system of God at all. He is drawn toward a closer coherency and compactness of thought; his religious convictions are comforted and fortified; he is better guarded, also, against fantastic experiences and wild illusions, that might otherwise confound the dignity of his life, and separate even his duties from the respect that is necessary to their value. No person will ever become, therefore, a good and sufficient teacher or preacher of the gospel, without a strong theologic discipline. But here, it will be seen, the benefit gained pertains principally to the building exercise, and not to the structure built. Possibly another system, differently shaped and colored, may temple as much of God's truth as mine; possibly other men want the exercise of building, too, more than a ready-built temple from me. Therefore, since God has given to his children so many blocks and timbers of words to be used in this good exercise, I will not complain that others of my friends are piling up very different looking structures from mine; but if they are built, as I can see, of the same material and so as to meet the same general use, I will then try to enjoy both theirs and mine together. Or, if they come upon me in anger, because my house is differently built from theirs, and call down fire from heaven to burn it, I will try to comfort myself in the confidence, that heaven has no fire, such as they ask for.

It is easy, also, to see that the instinct of system and a certain actual determination toward it are, in one view, necessary conditions of insight and true interpretation. We are forbidden thus to stop in the letter, and receive as truth a medly, or mere catalogue of symbols uninterpreted. We are required to observe and reduce their antagonisms, and, in order to this, to penetrate their forms and find the unity of truth in which they coalesce. Only we are in constant peril of setting one symbol, or class of symbols, above the others, and reducing these to system under the former, taken as being the literal truth; in which case they are virtually disallowed and rejected.

But if we speak of the actual results of theologic study and exercise,—the forms of truth, or opinion, or system prepared by it,—we need to distinguish between a close or merely reasoned system, and an open free system that waits for the discovery always of God; between an incrustation on the outside, to keep and imprison the life, and a cell or point of embryonic tissue begun at the center of life itself. They tell us that when the crustacea have grown a shell so thick and old that the life can no longer pierce through it and keep it on the footing of a living substance, it begins to be a foreign matter constraining the vital action, and the animal dies, suffocated by the tomb he has built. So it is when our theological crustacea are coffined in the close system we speak of. Since it is no longer *of* them, but a cerement of dead and strange matter *about* them, not quickened by their faith, they die of strange doctrine in it.

This distinction of a closed system and one that is open, between an incrustation and a vital embryonic center, will be farther cleared, perhaps, if it is stated as a distinction between mere theology and divinity.

Divinity has its basis in fact and being,—God as in the creation, God in history. It meets us in all outward objects; and again in the Scripture, in the form of political and religious annals, the biographies of distinguished saints, the teachings of prophets, the incarnate life and death of the Word made flesh. Here opens a vast realm of divine fact, radiant in every part with the light of God. But this all is body, not spirit; the face of divinity, but not the power. By divinity we mean what may be derived to us from this and made conscious within us, by an immediate experience of God, in connection with this. It is what of God a regenerate man may receive, in virtue of the new inner sense awakened in him. It is that influx and intergrowth of the divine nature that is consciously experienced, when every inlet of the soul is opened by love, and faith, and prayer, and holy living, and patient waiting upon God. It is interpretation made by experience,—a knowledge had of God, through the medium of consciousness, and resembling the knowledge we get of ourselves in the same manner; or, as I have said already, it is not a doctrine or system of doctrine, but a Living State, the Life of God in the soul of man. Of course it is an open state, and not a confined or closed state,—a condition of germinative force and ever extending growth.

Theology, on the other hand, according to the proper force of the word, in Greek, is what results, when the subject, God, is logically expounded or reasoned. What the result will be depends, of course, on the state or point where the exposition begins. If the operator stands in the position of a simply natural consciousness, then he expounds what he has included in his consciousness. This may be called *mere* theology, a science built without divine experience, as one might give a theoretic account of the moon's atmosphere without having breathed it. Or, if the operator begin at the point of a living consciousness of God, which is the state of real divinity, then his effort will be to expound that in speculative order, just as the intellectual philosopher expounds his intellectual consciousness. This may be called *Christian* theology, or evangelical theology; or it is sometimes called divinity; though it will be undivine, just according to the degree of human defect or mistake there is in it, which is probably a large subtraction. . . .*

---

* [Ed.] Elsewhere in *Christ in Theology* (pp. 84–86), Bushnell associates his conviction that "Christian consciousness" is the proper ground for theology with similar views put forth by Richard Rothe (1799–1867), a German theologian strongly influenced by Schleiermacher. Bushnell knew of Rothe's work only from a brief translation appended to John D. Morell's *Philosophy of Religion* (New York: D. Appleton & Co., 1849). However, his immediate, sympathetic response to Rothe shows how closely Bushnell was attuned to

At the same time, it does not follow, either that philosophy or theology is worthless. They have an immense value as exercises and cultivating powers, although so little able to fix and settle in words the import of our consciousness, or to produce the system of the infinite in which alone our consciousness can have its full interpretation. There is a progress in theology, due as much to its varieties, as to the excellence of its particular determinations. It is even useful or necessary, as a re-acting basis for the mind, in climbing into a divine experience. If it is so blended with that experience, as to have its light therein, and be corrected and amplified thereby as an open system; if it is catholic in the same, as acknowledging all other systems based upon the same Scripture foundation; in a word, if it is saturated with divinity, so as to be divinity according to the true force of that word, formerly so current, but latterly so far displaced, then it is the true wisdom of God. Not all wisdom, but true; for still there is a livelier and more competent medium of truth than any that classes in the modes of speculation; I mean the medium of simple expression. The poetic forms of utterance are closer to the fires of religion within us, more adequate revelations of consciousness, because they reveal it in flame. Parable, symbol, description, illustration, emphasis and tone, the look of a divine charity and the conduct of a soul in the divine beauty,—these, I hope you will agree, are better and more adequate revelations of truth than theology, in its best form, can be.

---

the currents of international theological liberalism. For a more complete exposition of Bushnell's understanding of Christian consciousness, see "The Immediate Knowledge of God," *Sermons on Living Subjects* (New York: Scribner, Armstrong & Co., 1872), pp. 114–28.

# "THE WORDING FORTH OF GOD:"
## INCARNATION AND TRINITY

From *Christ in Theology*,
"The Person of Christ" (1851)*

Passing now from this general view of language and doctrine, or of theologic method, to some of the particular topics of my book,†—the Person of Christ, the Trinity, and the Work of Redemption,—it will be seen that all my supposed heresies, in reference to these great subjects, are caused by the arrest of speculation and the disallowance of those constructive judgments, or a priori arguments, by which terms that are only analogies, and mysteries that are most significant when taken only as symbols, are made to affirm something wiser and more exact than what they express. It is very easy for a critic, who wishes to be sharp against me at the smallest expense of steel, to please himself in the discovery that I am only trying in fact, without knowing it, to introduce a new dogmatism. This, I believe, is the turn that several have given to their strictures. And about an equal number have charged, directly opposite to these, that I propose to throw down all the pillars of theology, break up all the solid foundations of truth, and commend every one to the liberty of his own passions, and the vagaries of his own imagination. It will be found that I am doing exactly neither,—that I am simply cutting short speculation at the point where it begins to *create* a knowledge by inference, and transferring the matter that was going to be preyed upon by logic, directly into the care of spiritual discernment, the only qualified interpreter,—there to be felt, experienced, fed upon, as the true bread, before it has become so mixed with dialectic quibbles and scientific unwisdoms, that it has no longer any bread or nutriment to yield. It will be found that, instead of trying to get all the great truths in question, *out of* their symbols into others, and build them into sciences that are independent of the symbols, I am rather showing how to stay by the symbols or in them, as the best and holiest expressions of truth; on the ground that Christian doctrine is most adequately distinguished in

* [Ed.] *Christ in Theology* (Hartford: Brown and Parsons, 1851), pp. 90–116. Included here: pp. 90–94, 99–100.
† [Ed.] *God in Christ*.

the forms of the word, by a devout inspection or perusal of them, taken as simple presentations; just as the souls of our friends are presented in, and expressed by, and not argued inferentially from, or *out of* their bodies.

It will be seen that I have managed, in this way, to find a place for faith that is freer and more simple, and just as much more intelligent. In regard to each of the three subjects, it will be seen that nothing is done save simply to show how the forms in which God is offered to our faith may be *used* so as to get their true meaning and be themselves the truth to us. The fundamental principle assumed is this and no other,—that the value of the word rests in the impressions it is to produce in us, and not in the theories or scientific versions we are to produce of it. . . .

This will now be seen, as I proceed to exhibit, more fully and carefully, the doctrine I designed to assert, in reference to the three principal subjects of revelation just named. I begin with the Person of Christ.

Who is Christ? The incarnation of the divine nature. For what purpose? The manifestation of God—therefore he is called the Life manifested—God manifest in the flesh—the Word made flesh, that we may behold in him the Father's glory—the express image of God—God in Christ reconciling the world unto himself. In his miraculous birth, too, he is seen to be of a double nature, at once divine and human, the Son of God and the Son of Mary.

Two things then are evident. First, that he is a very peculiar being, who can not be classed in the simple genus humanity; in one view a union of the incompatible, the divine and the human, the infinite and the finite; and being thus a person wholly abnormal and mysterious, we manifestly can not interpret the language applied to him by a reference to our own merely normal experience or consciousness, and so make out the internal mystery of his nature. If sometimes acts are attributed to him that seem to be divine, sometimes others that seem to be human, we can not say, 'this infers deity,' 'this a human soul;' we can only refer them all alike to the one abnormal person and the secret mystery of his consciousness. Secondly, it is to be seen beforehand that he is not given as a riddle to our curiosity or that we may set ourselves to reason out his mystery, but simply that God may thus express his own feeling and draw himself into union with us, by an act of accommodation to our human sympathies and capacities.

But the question remains, who is Christ, what is there in him? The true answer is, that he is, externally viewed, a union of God and man, whose object is to humanize the conception of God, and so to express or communicate God. But is there any distinct human soul in the person of Christ? What are the contents of his person? Here begins one of my heresies, when I answer that the question is impracticable, unphilosophic, dictated only by false curiosity, and of course not answered by scripture. Christ is here to express God, not to puzzle us in questions about the internal composition of his person. Besides, the human element is nothing to me, save as it brings me God, or discovers to me, a sinner, the patience and brotherhood of God, as a Redeemer from sin. As to the man, the human soul, I see men enough and meet with human souls enough elsewhere. The tenderness we rejoice in, as testified in the person of Christ and under the type of a human feeling, is the tenderness of God, not the tenderness of the human soul, or of the distinct human substance of Jesus. What we feel so deeply is that God is with us, on our human level, and is drawn so close to our sympathy—not that a man is. And the moment we find a human soul in him, distinctly conscious and distinctly active, we shall immediately draw ourselves to that, in the manner of the mere humanitarians, and having our sympathy with that, we shall be turned quite away from what is the sole, or, at least, principal object of the incarnation; viz., the manifestation of the Life, or the expression of God. . . .

However, the orthodox formula—"two natures and one person"—is correctly worded, if only it be taken in the more exterior, and not in the analytical and speculative sense. We are to regard him as a person representable to thought only by means of two poles, or denominations, the divine and the human; which, however, we can no way investigate, as regards the mode of their interior relation; which, in one view, are wholly incompatible. The object of the mystery is not to raise a scientific problem, but to express God. Our wisdom, therefore, is to receive him, in perfect simplicity, as a twofold nature, a person who is God with us, Son of God and Son of Man; and holding him before us, by these two poles of thought, to let him have just that power in the soul and bring in just that sense of God and union to God, which he will, when thus regarded. That he is divine, the Word made flesh, we know; for that is revealed. That the transaction is properly described, not as a coming together and spiritual coalescence of the Word and some man, but as an assumption of humanity or the flesh, we also know. But whether the assumption included the assumption of a human soul; or whether, if it does and that soul lapses into the divine person so as to have, no more, any personality or character of its own, it would really *be*; or so far different from the state of not being, that a true account of the one person would require us to notice at all the presence, or trace the historic fortunes of an entity so ambiguous,—what, in a word, the assumption involves, how the one person thus resulting is interiorly constituted, what part the human occupies in him or is, who speaks, obeys, suffers, dies,— these are questions we are never to raise. They are by the supposition excluded, both as being impossible and irrelevant. We have nothing to do but simply to look upon the incidents of the life of Jesus as belonging to the one divine person and, through these incidents, taken all as media of divine expression, come, as directly as possible, into the import and power of what is expressed.*

* [Ed.] Bushnell, taking his own advice here, frequently tried to show the self-evident divinity of Jesus through a simple review of his life and character. His best known effort along these lines was Chapter X of *Nature and the Supernatural*, subsequently published separately as *The Character of Jesus: Forbidding his Possible Classification with Men* (New York: Charles Scribner, 1861).

## From *God in Christ*, "Concio ad Clerum: A Discourse on the Divinity of Christ" (1849)*

Observe that, when God is revealed, it cannot be as the One, as the Infinite, or Absolute, but only as through media. And as there are no infinite media, no signs that express the infinite, no minds, in fact, that can apprehend the infinite by direct inspection, the One must appear in the manifold; the Absolute in the conditional; Spirit in form; the Motionless in motion; the Infinite in the finite. He must distribute Himself, He must let forth His nature in sounds, colors, forms, works, definite objects and signs. It must be to us as if Brama were waking up; as if Jehovah, the Infinite I am, the Absolute, were dividing off Himself into innumerable activities that shall dramatize His immensity, and bring Him within the molds of language and discursive thought. And in whatever thing He appears, or is revealed, there will be something that misrepresents, as well as something that represents Him. The revealing process, that which makes Him appear, will envelope itself in clouds of formal contradiction—that is, of diction which is contrary, in some way, to the truth, and which, taken simply as diction, is continually setting forms against each other.

Thus, the God revealed, in distinction from the God Absolute, will have parts, forms, colors, utterances, motions, activities, assigned Him. He will think, deliberate, reason, remember, have emotions. Then, taking up all these manifold representations, casting out the matter in which they are cross to each other, and repugnant to the very idea of the God they represent, we shall settle into the true knowledge of God, and receive, as far as the finite can receive the Infinite, the contents of the divine nature. . . .

To make this same view yet more evident, observe that we ourselves being finite, under time and succession, reasoning, deliberating, thinking, remembering, having emotions, can never come into the knowledge of God, save as God is brought within our finite molds of action. There are certain absolute verities which belong to our own nature, and which, therefore, we can know as absolute, or which, I should rather say, we must know. They are such as the ideas of space, cause, truth, right, and

* [Ed.] *God in Christ* (Hartford: Brown and Parsons, 1849), pp. 121–81. Included here: 139–48, 173–75.

the axioms of mathematical science. But these are simple ideas, and have their reality in us. God is a BEING out of us, a Being in whom the possibilities and even facts of all other being have their spring. Taken in this view, as the absolute, all-comprehensive being, we can know Him only *as* being; that is, by a revelation, or rather by revelations, giving out one after another, and in one way or another, but always in finite forms, something that belongs to the knowledge of God. And then we know God only as we bring all our knowledges together. Thus we approach the knowledge of the Absolute Being, and there is no other way possible, or even conceivable. . . .

Now it is in this manner only, through relations, contrasts, actions and reactions, that we come into the knowledge of God. As Absolute Being, we know Him not. But our mind, acted under the law of action and reaction, is carried up to Him, or thrown back upon Him, to apprehend Him more and more perfectly. Nothing that we see, or can see, represents Him fully, or can represent Him truly; for the finite cannot show us the Infinite. But between various finites, acting so as to correct each other, and be supplements to each other, we get a true knowledge. Our method may be compared to that of resultant motions in philosophy. No one finite thing represents the Absolute Being; but between two or more finite forces acting obliquely on our mind, it is driven out, in a resultant motion, towards the Infinite. Meantime, a part of the two finite forces, being oblique or false, is destroyed by the mutual counteraction of forces.

Under this same law, I suggest that we look for a solution of the trinity, and of the person of Jesus Christ. They are relatives, to conduct us up to the Absolute. . . .

We go back, now, to the Absolute Being, to consider by what process He will be revealed, and to see that revelation unfolded. And here I must bring to view a singular and eminent distinction of the Divine nature, without which He could never be revealed.

There is in God, taken as the Absolute Being, a capacity of self-expression, so to speak, which is peculiar—a generative power of form, a creative imagination, in which, or by aid of which, He can produce Himself outwardly, or represent Himself in the finite. In this respect, God is wholly unlike to us. Our imagination is passive, stored with forms, colors and types of words from without, borrowed from the world we live in. But all such forms, God has in Himself, and this is the Logos, the Word, elsewhere called the Form of God. Now, this Word, this Form of God, in which He sees Himself, is with God, as John says, from the beginning. It is God mirrored before His own understanding, and to be mirrored, as in fragments of the mirror, before us. Conceive Him now as creating the worlds, or creating worlds, if you please, from eternity. In so doing, He only represents, expresses, or outwardly produces Himself.

He bodies out His own thoughts. What we call the creation, is, in another view, a revelation only of God, His first revelation.

And it is in this view that the Word, or Logos, elsewhere called Christ, or the Son of God, is represented as the Creator of the worlds. Or it is said, which is only another form of the same truth, that the worlds were made by or through him, and the apostle John adds, that without Him, is not anything made that was made. Now, as John also declares, there was light, the first revelation was made, God was expressed in the forms and relations of the finite. But the light shined in darkness, and the darkness comprehended it not. The divine Word was here; he had come to his own, but his own received him not. One thing more is possible that will yield a still more effulgent light, viz: that, as God has produced Himself in all the other finite forms of being, so now he should appear in the human.

Indeed, He has appeared in the human before, in the same way as He has in all the created objects of the world. The human person, taken as a mere structure, adapted to the high uses of intelligence and moral action, is itself a noble illustration of His wisdom, and a token also of the exalted and good purposes cherished in our existence. But there was yet more of God to be exhibited in the Human Form of our race. As the spirit of man is made in the image of God, and his bodily form is prepared to be the fit vehicle and outward representative of his spirit, it follows that his bodily form has also some inherent, a priori relation to God's own nature; such probably as makes it the truest, most expressive finite type of Him. Continuing, therefore, in a pure upright character, our whole race would have been a visible revelation of the truth and beauty of God. But having not thus continued, having come under the power of evil, that which was to be the expression, or reflection of God, became appropriated to the expression of evil. Truth has no longer any living unblemished manifestation in the world; the beauty of goodness lives and smiles no more. Sin, prejudice, passion,—stains of every color— so deface and mar the race, that the face of God, the real glory of the Divine, is visible no longer. Now, therefore, God will reclaim this last type of Himself, possess it with His own life and feeling, and through that, live Himself into the acquaintance and biographic history of the world. "And the word was made flesh, and dwelt among us; and we beheld his glory as of the only begotten of the Father, full of grace and truth." "The only begotten Son, which is in the bosom of the Father, he hath declared Him."* This is Christ whose proper deity or divinity we have proved.

Prior to this moment, there has been no appearance of trinity in the

---

* [Ed.] These quotes and other references in the preceding paragraph are all from the first chapter of the gospel of John.

revelations God has made of His being; but just here, whether as result-ing from the incarnation or as implied in it, we are not informed, a three-fold personality or impersonation of God begins to offer itself to view. Just here, accordingly, as the revelation culminates or completes the fullness of its form, many are staggered and confused by difficulties which they say are contrary to reason—impossible therefore to faith. I think otherwise. In these three persons or impersonations I only see a revelation of the Absolute Being, under just such relatives as by their mutual play, in and before our imaginative sense, will produce in us the truest knowledge of God—render Him most conversable, bring Him closest to feeling, give Him the freest, least obstructed access, as a quick-ening power, to our hearts. . . .

Thus we have three persons, or impersonations, all existing under finite conditions or conceptions. They are relatives, and, in that view, are not infinites; for relative infinites are impossible. And yet, taken repre-sentatively, they are each and all, infinites; because they stand for, and express the Infinite, Absolute Jehovah. They may each declare, 'I am He;' for what they impart to us of Him, is their true reality. Between them all together, as relatives, we are elevated to proximity and virtual converse with Him who is above our finite conditions,—the Unapproach-able, and, as far as all measures of thought or conception are concerned, the Unrepresentable God.

The Father plans, presides and purposes for us; the Son expresses his intended mercy, proves it, brings it down even to the level of a fellow-feeling; the Spirit works within us the beauty he reveals, and the glory beheld in his Life. The Father sends the Son, the Son delivers the grace of the Father; the Father dispenses, and the Son procures the Spirit; the Spirit proceeds from the Father and Son, to fulfill the purpose of one, and the expressed feeling of the other; each and all together dramatize and bring forth into life about us that Infinite One, who, to our mere thought, were no better than Brama sleeping on eternity and the stars. Now, the sky, so to speak, is beginning to be full of Divine Activities, heaven is married to earth, and earth to heaven, and the Absolute Jehovah, whose nature we before could nowise comprehend, but dimly know, and yet more dimly feel, has, by these outgoings, waked up in us, all living images of His love and power and presence, and set the whole world in a glow. . . .

Do you then ask, whether I mean simply to assert a modal trinity, or three modal persons?—I must answer obscurely, just as I answered in regard to the humanity of Christ. If I say that they are modal only, as the word is commonly used, I may deny more than I am justified in denying, or am required to deny, by the ground I have taken. I will only say that the trinity, or the three persons, are given to me for the sake of their external expression, not for the internal investigation of their contents. If I use them rationally or wisely, then, I shall use them according to their object. I must not intrude upon their interior nature, either by assertion or denial. They must have their reality to me in what they express when taken as the wording forth of God. Perhaps I shall come nearest to the simple, positive idea of the trinity here maintained, if I call it an INSTRUMENTAL TRINITY, and the persons INSTRUMENTAL PERSONS. There may be more in them than this, which let others declare when they find it. Enough, meantime, for me, that there is this;—that in and through these living persons, or impersonations, I find the Infinite One brought down even to my own level of humanity, without any loss of His greatness, or reduction of His majesty.

From *Christ in Theology*,
"The Trinity" (1851)*


It seems to be supposed by many that what I advanced concerning the trinity, in my discourse at New Haven,† was designed to be a solution of this great mystery. Precisely contrary to this, my attempt was to find a way of intelligent repose in it without a solution, and even subject to the conviction that no proper solution is possible. I did indeed seek to account for the external fact of trinity, showing that when God, the Absolute One, is revealed to us—the infinite in the finite, spirit in form, or subject, as the nature of language itself requires, to conditions of form—the process involves a necessity of antagonistic symbols and, if there be an incarnation, pluralities of person, such as meet us in the trinity of the New Testament. But having thus accounted for the external fact of a trinity, taken as instrumental in respect to the revelation of God, I insisted that we have now come to the last limit of possible investigation; that we can not pass over into the divine nature itself and show how the instrumental three of revelation are related to its interior distribution, or precisely what they affirm concerning it. Probably their object is, under and by means of the manifold, to give us the One, or to show us the One as engaged in forms of action needful to our redemption from sin; not to inform us concerning the transcendent properties and distributions of the divine substance as related to problems of metaphysical science. Probably the revelation thus offered us in the Christian trinity has a considerable part of its value, in the fact that it can not be definitely solved, and sets Him before us under a veil of mystery; for, as nothing that is infinite can be definite, so mystery is a necessary dynamic of expression for the infinite.

Just here, too, in withholding from any attempt to solve the trinity, and refusing either to affirm or to deny any thing concerning it, as pertaining to the substance or the immanent properties of God, is the peculiarity—the merit if there is any, the heresy if there is none—of the exposition I have ventured to offer. It differs, in this view, from Sabellianism on one side, and

* [Ed.] *Christ in Theology* (Hartford: Brown and Parsons), pp. 117–211. Included here: 117–24, 126–27.

† [Ed.] Bushnell is referring to the address "Concio ad Clerum," delivered at Yale in 1848, published in *God in Christ*, and excerpted immediately above in this volume.

common orthodoxy on the other, in the same manner, being an attempt to forestall the controversy between them; a controversy that is endless, for the simple reason that the subject of it is impossible. In the same way, it proposes to anticipate and cut off nearly all the opposing theories of trinity, heretical and otherwise, that have agitated so deeply the peace of the church; for they all arise from the attempt to settle a conception of trinity as pertaining immanently to the interior nature of God—an attempt, the certain futility of which, it would seem that a very little reflection might assist any one to discover.

I spoke, in my Introduction, of a certain coincidence between the view of trinity I advanced at New Haven, and that of Schleiermacher, in his exposition of Sabellius;* and some have supposed, I perceive, that I meant to accept, with him, the doctrine of a modal trinity. I ought to have traced the limits of the coincidence and shown precisely where my doctrine escapes the charge of modalism. Thus, if it is set in comparison with Schleiemacher's on one side, and the orthodox modification of it demanded by Prof. Stuart on the other, it will be found that we have three different schemes of trinity, which begin together, at the assumed fact of God's original unity, and then, by a consideration of what is involved in revealing Him to men, or working the redemption of men, arrive at the resulting fact of a trinity—three grammatic persons, Father, Son, and Holy Ghost, representing, all, to our human conception, the *Homoousion*, or One Substance. Meeting at this point, we immediately fall asunder into results that are mutually repugnant.

Schleiermacher and his translator both assume the possibility of entering into the interior nature of God, and forming an authorized judgment concerning the trinity as predicable of it. This I deny, and am thus left behind by them both. The judgment of the German critic is that the One becomes Three in the process of revelation, and that the Three are *only* media of revelation. This is modalism. His translator, on the other hand, argues that, since God is revealed as being three, he must be essentially or immanently three back of the revelation; else the revelation would not be true. This is admitted orthodoxy. . . .

Left behind thus by them both, I am found simply protesting against

---

* [Ed.] Bushnell's treatment of the trinity was influenced by Schleiermacher's "On the Discrepancy Between the Sabellian and Athanasian Method of Representing the Doctrine of the Trinity," translated and published with extensive notes and commentary by Moses Stuart in the *Biblical Repository and Quarterly Review*, V (April 1835), pp. 265–353; and VI (July 1835), pp. 1–116. On the issue of Bushnell's Sabellian sympathies, see Fred Kirschenmann, "Horace Bushnell: Orthodox or Sabellian?" *Church History*, XXXII (March 1964), pp. 49–59. Kirschenmann, like most recent commentators, acknowledges Bushnell's substantial orthodoxy. For an excellent analysis of Bushnell's theory in its New England context, see Donald Crosby, *Horace Bushnell's Theory of Language* (The Hague: Mouton, 1975), pp. 179–228.

all judgments and inferences that undertake to leap the gulf between us and the inscrutable mystery of God, insisting that we stay by the Scripture and trust ourselves to *no* constructive reasonings on the subject,— that the trinity of revelation is given us for use and not for theory; that we can not know exactly where form ends, or how much to refer to form, in a matter so transcendent; that any attempt to solve or conceive God's interior mystery, by reasonings cast in the molds and categories of our human consciousness, is presumptuous, possibly even absurd; and attempt, also, to clear that mystery, which it may have been one of the very objects of Scripture to present, as being itself the medium and highest power of expression for the infinite. Therefore, I said, let us stay by the simple Three of revelation, receiving them, not as addressed to our scientific instinct, but under the simple conditions of expression; sending and sent, acting and interacting, so, by their discursive method, meeting our discourse of thought, and communicating, by their accommodation to our capacity, what they may of the divine glory and love.

You perceive, in this manner, that my supposed heresy is distinguished, in the same way, both from modalism and immanent trinity. One enters into the field of God's interior nature and denies, the other enters and affirms. I have supposed it to be a demand even of reason, and certainly to be more modest, to withhold altogether; seeking after God in the simple *use* of that by which he is offered to knowledge. The incurious method I have supposed to be more intelligent here than the curious, the practical than the speculative; that feeling and imagination are sometimes good interpreters and proper inlets of knowledge; and that we are never so likely to miss the true import of this transcendent mystery, as when we are thrusting ourselves into God's interior distributions, and preparing a psychology of his Infinite Spirit in the tiny molds of our discursive understanding.

The advantages pertaining to such a disposition of the subject are many.

First, it is a solution, just so far as a solution is wanted. It finds reason to believe, assuming the strict unity of God, that He will be revealed under conditions of form and number; the Absolute by relatives, or, in case of an incarnation, by relative persons. Then, when the scripture trinity appears, the disciple is not shocked by a raw absurdity thrust upon Him. This trinity, coupled with so many speculative difficulties, is at least no proof against the fact of a revelation; for it is just what might be expected, in case a revelation is made. He has also perceived that a trinity of persons thus appearing is developed, one side of mere logical conditions, and is not to be handled by logical deductions. As soon, therefore, as men cease to be occupied with the relative subjects, or persons, as media of expression,—presentations of God to simple faith and love,—and begin to raise a priori constructions on their formal relations of act, and work, and number, he clearly perceives that there should be and will be no end to the conflicts and resulting contrarieties of doctrine that appear, and will not be troubled, of course, by them, when they do appear. The unity of God is to him a truth fixed and immovable, and he is not concerned lest, in receiving as much of God as he can through the revelation given, he should somehow accept a logical absurdity. He has only to receive the Divine Three in terms of love and worship, using them freely as media of thought concerning God and the way of His redeeming mercy, and so to ascend, through formulas of blessing and doxologies of praise, to the fullest embrace possible of the incomprehensible One.

Secondly, it is another advantage of the view I have suggested that, while it holds the mind to a practical use of the trinity, it allows and provokes to the highest activity of thought concerning God. Nothing strains the human mind to such tensity as a riddle or mystery, when that riddle or mystery is not a fiction, but is based in the depth of some stupendous reality. And for just this reason it is that the trinity of Scripture has availed to make the nature of God a problem of so great interest to the human mind for the last eighteen centuries. Such a strain of human thought after God and his transcendent mystery could have been kept up by no other means. And the result has been that, while nothing has been gained as regards the real comprehension or solution of the mystery—that while so many heresies and confutations and determinations of councils, so much labor of logic and scholastic learning, so many divinations of mysticism, so many theories of ontology and transcendental philosophy, have ended in just no solution or doctrine of the subject that can hope for general acceptance—there has yet resulted such a lifting of the range and such an expansion of the circle of thought concerning God, as more than compensates the immense labor it has cost. The very confusion we complain of is, in one view, but another name for fertility. And what we have thus attained, we should never have begun to seek, had only the simple Jewish conception of divine unity been given us. We owe it all to the amazing riddle thrown out to the mind of the world, in the Christian trinity. And it is one of the highest merits of the Christian expression of God under a threefold personality, that it would not allow the mind of the world to rest any longer in a conception so easy to thought and, in fact, so nearly finite; but compelled a new toil of exploration, and thus conducted to a new sense of the possibilities included in God and the mystery of infinite being.

Now, the effort of the church has been and still is, though not so intended, to stop exactly that which it has been the merit of the Scripture trinity to be doing. Could some science of the trinity, or of God's immanent distribution, be perfected and established in a fixed form of dogma, so that nothing more would be left us but to run over the logical terms and hear what they say, then manifestly the labor of the world's mind would rest and the process of fertility be ended. And not only so, not only would God never be greater to thought, but there would begin to be a wave of retrocession, a subsidence of thought to a lower level. Since the dogma is, in that case, an end of question, thought receives it without question; and then, having God by rote, He becomes to mind as lifeless as mind is lifeless to Him; as much diminished in volume, too, as thought is diminished in the strain of its intensity. Accordingly, just that is wanted, which the church has been trying, in all ages, to escape, viz., to keep the trinity an open question forever,—precisely where the scriptures leave it,—to undertake no science of God's interior nature and immanent properties, but to hold the Sacred Three as instrumental verities, the truest and most adequate expression of God's reality possible; leaving room for thought to make its explorations and climb into the knowledge of God by such feeling after his mystery, as mystery will tempt, and freedom suffer, and faith assist. Precisely this is the position where my doctrine leaves us; and, in this, it has its advantage equally over modalism and orthodoxy, and all ontological and transcendental theories. . . .

Here we come upon the proper domain of mystery, having a perfectly intelligent knowledge prepared to its locality and its confines. We are not simply overtaken by darkness, or driven to a corner whence we can not escape, save by calling on Mystery to help us; but we meet her in the place of intelligence, and greet her as an acquaintance. For we have seen beforehand that the relation of form to truth in every term of language is a mystery quite insoluble, and now we only meet a particular example of the same fact. We perceive, too, beforehand, that the infinite, when revealed in the finite, must be enveloped in mystery. Besides, the nature of God is different from ours, in such a sense that we manifestly can not form the interior conception of God as the One, and never can tell how much of threeness to refer to the vehicle, in distinction from the reality signified. The categories of the Infinite Mind are not matched by the categories of thought in ours; and therefore, when we affirm God's oneness, we have no certainty how much it includes, but only that all is included in one consciousness. It may be that, in certain respects, it would be closer to the reality for us to affirm an interior threeness in God, than to say that he is a simple unity in our strictly *human* sense, or the sense of our finite personality. It certainly is more true for us, to take the Three as they are offered, and let them throw us into a maze by their cross relations; and in that maze, if we are in it in faith, longing only to be filled with God, we shall receive the largest possible communication of Him, as a being who can not be placed in the categories of our finite understanding. We shall have Him thus dynamically, or in virtual impression, when we can not make out a proper intellectual conception of Him. Here, then, when we come to the question, what is vehicle and what is truth, we neither affirm nor deny; but we say, here is the place for mystery, and she meets us only where the place for meeting is. We are not offended; we receive her gladly; perceiving in her shaded face and lineaments that, as she is the mother of Modesty, she is the sister also of Truth.

# From "The Christian Trinity a Practical Truth" (1854)*

Thus far, it will be remarked, we have nothing to do with the interior mystery of the divine nature. The argument amounts to nothing more than that God, even assuming his strict unity, must needs be *exhibited* in this way, in order to the uses stated. Finding a certain threefold designation of God given out in the Christian Scriptures, in which he is presented, in form, as three personalities, Father, Son, and Holy Ghost, we take up the subject at this point and show that, taken as means of divine representation, they are necessary to the adequate impression of God, and the practical uses of a supernatural and redemptive economy.

But the question will be raised by many, at this point, whether after all, there is anything in God answering to these personalities? Some Unitarian, for example, having followed us to just this point and admitted the force of our argument, may require to be informed wherein the truth or reality of the triune formula consists, or what there is in God's nature to support these personalities of revelation? And to this we might well enough reply by handing back the question. Having shown the practical need of just what the Scripture gives, it is not therefore specially incumbent on us to settle all other and deeper questions that may be raised. . . .

But we will not so dismiss the question, lest by an evasion of responsibility, at the point reached, we may seem to regard the Trinity as a matter only of words, and not in any proper sense an eternal fact. . . .

What then shall we say of this tri-personality acted by God? What account shall we make of it? Is it that God will accommodate himself in this manner to finite minds? That would reduce the Trinity to an occasional matter, a voluntary expedient; which would be a supposition as painful and quite as remote from all our most earnest convictions as to believe that his personality is a merely occasional matter, an act of voluntary accommodation to our finite apprehensions, and not any part of his eternal property or idea.

What then is it that gives us the impression, when we speak of God's personality, that it is an eternal property in him, a something which appertains to the divine idea itself? It cannot be that he exists as an infinite

* [Ed.] *The New Englander*, XII (1854), pp. 485–509. Republished in *Building Eras in Religion* (New York: Charles Scribner's Sons, 1881), pp. 106–149. Included here, from *Building Eras*: pp. 131–36.

substance in the mold of our human personality; it cannot be that there is a *core* of literal personality wrapped up in his infinite substance. It is not enough that he acts personality in a way of voluntary accommodation to men. It can be only that by some *interior necessity*, he is thus accommodated in his action to the finite; for what he does by the necessity of his nature as truly pertains to his idea, and is as truly inherent in him, as if it were the form of his divine substance itself. And precisely here we come upon the Nicene Trinity. This and all the formulas of Trinity that assert the "eternal generation," affirm the unity of the persons as a unity of substance,—*homoousioi*, "same in substance"; and then regarding the eternal going on, so to speak, of God, his living process or act, *actus purissimus*, they find him eternally threeing himself, or generating three persons. These documents do not mean that God, at some date in his almanac called eternity, begat his Son and sent forth his Holy Spirit; but that in some high sense undefinable, he is datelessly and eternally becoming three, or by a certain inward necessity being accommodated in his action to the categories of finite apprehension, adjusted to that as that to the receiving of his mystery.*

This necessary act of God is sometimes illustrated by a reference to our necessary action, in the process of consciousness. Thus in simply being conscious, which we are, not by act of will, but by force of simply being what we are, we first take note of ourselves; secondly, raise a conception or thought of ourselves; and thirdly, recognize the correspondence of that conception with ourselves. And this we do as long as we exist, and because we exist. And some have gone so far as even to discover, in this fact, a parallel and a real explication of the Trinity of God. The illustration is reliable however, only as a demonstration of the intensely inherent character of all necessary action. Were this three-folding of consciousness a matter of substance, it would not be more truly inherent than it is, regarded as an act.

If then we dare to assume what is the deepest, most adorable fact of God's nature, that he is a being infinite, *inherently related in act* to the finite, otherwise impossible ever to be found in that relation, thus and therefore a being who is everlastingly threeing himself in his action, to be and to be known as Father, Son, and Holy Ghost from eternity to eternity, we are brought out full upon the Christian Trinity, and that in the simple line of practical inquiry itself. It is nothing but the doctrine

---

* [Ed.] Bushnell confessed in 1851 that at the time he wrote his seminal treatment of the trinity in *God in Christ*, he "had not sufficiently conceived [the Nicene Creed's] import, or the title it has to respect as a Christian document." Nevertheless, he insisted that his own views simply "reproduced, in a different form, what is really the substantial import of that doctrine." (*Christ in Theology* [Hartford: Brown and Parsons, 1851], p. 177.) His later discussions of the doctrine—such as the one here—show greater respect for the classical formulas, but do not significantly alter his original position.

that *God is a being practically related to his creatures.* And for just this reason it was that Christ, in the commission given to his disciples, set forth his formula of Trinity as a comprehensive designation for the gospel, and a revelation of the everlasting ground it has in the inherent properties of God. He calls it therein as emphatically as possible his "everlasting gospel," a work as old as the Trinity of God, a valid and credible work, because it is based in the Trinity of God. So glorious and high, and yet so nigh is God; related in all that is inmost, more inherent in his nature and eternity, to our finite want, and the double kingdom of nature and grace, by which we are to be raised up and perfected for the skies: a being who is at once absolute and relational; an all-containing, all-supporting Unity, and a manifolding humanly personal love; the All in all itself, and yet *above* all, *through* all, and *in* all; *of* whom also, and *through* whom, and *to* whom be glory forever.

# From "Our Gospel a Gift to the Imagination" (1869)*

Thus if God is to be himself revealed, he has already thrown out symbols for it, filling the creation full of them, and these will all be played into metaphor. The day will be his image, the sea, the great rock's shadow, the earthquake, the dew, the fatherhood care of the child, and the raven and the feeble folk of the conies,—all that the creation is and contains, in all depths and heights and latitudes and longitudes of space,—everything expresses God by some image that is fit, as far as it goes. "Day unto day uttereth speech, and night unto night showeth knowledge."† Metaphor on metaphor crowds the earth and the skies, bearing each a face that envisages the Eternal Mind, whose word or wording forth it is to be. Again he takes a particular people into covenant specially with himself, just in order to make their public history the Providential metaphor, so to speak, of his rulership and redeeming teachership, leading them on and about by his discipline, and raising light and shade as between them and the world-kingdoms of the false gods about them, to set himself in relief as the true Lord of all. And then, following still the same law of expression by outward fact and image, he crowns the revelation process by the incarnate life and life-story of his Son, erecting on earth a supernatural kingdom to govern the world in the interest of his supernatural redemption. And if we do not take the word in some light, frivolous, merely rhetorician way, we can say nothing of Christ so comprehensively adequate as to call him the metaphor of God; God's last metaphor! And when we have gotten all the metaphoric meanings of his life and death, all that is expressed and bodied in his person of God's saving help and new-creating, sin-forgiving, reconciling love, the sooner we dismiss all speculations on the literalities of his incarnate miracles, his derivation, the composition of his person, his suffering,—plainly transcendent as regards our possible understanding,—the wiser shall we be in our discipleship. We shall have him as the express image of God's person. We shall have "the light of the knowledge of the glory of God, in the face of Jesus Christ."‡ Beholding

* [Ed.] *Hours at Home*, X (December 1869), pp. 159–72. Republished in *Building Eras in Religion* (New York: Charles Scribner's Sons, 1881), pp. 249–85. Included here, from *Building Eras*: pp. 258–60.
† [Ed.] Psalm 19:2.
‡ [Ed.] II Corinthians 4:6. This verse was later used as the text of a sermon preached by

in him as in a glass the glory of the Lord, we shall be changed into the same image.* The metaphoric contents are ours, and beyond that nothing is given.

Bushnell for Washington Gladden's ordination service. See "The Gospel of the Face," *Sermons on Living Subjects* (New York: Scribner, Armstrong & Co., 1872), pp. 73–95.

  * [Ed.] The phrase echoes II Corinthians 3:18, another favorite verse of Bushnell's. See "Unconscious Influence" below.

# PART II

# THE NEW LIFE: SYMBOLISM AND GROWTH

# THE NEW LIFE: SYMBOLISM AND GROWTH

> But we all with open face beholding as in a glass i.e. in Christ the
> glory of the Lord are changed into the same image from glory to
> glory.
> —Bushnell, "Christ the Form of the Soul"

Bushnell's theory of language culminates in a vision of the power of language to shape human moral character and ultimately to communicate the Life of God to mankind. Bushnell understood language primarily as a vehicle for conveying inward states from mind to mind. We express ourselves outwardly, and those who understand us take the *im*pression of what we *ex*press, recapitulating our inwardness. In effect, then, human inwardness is constantly being shared through the medium of expression. Society is organic; we "flow together" in all our interactions. Every person's character makes itself felt in society as a shaping power. Similarly, every symbolic expression has a power to influence the growth of receptive minds.

Bushnell stated these principles of social psychology concisely in the sermon "Unconscious Influence" (1846). The writings presented along with it here under the heading "Nurture and the Supernatural" take up the implications of this theory for the practical life of religion, especially with regard to Christian education. In "Growth Not Conquest the True Method of Christian Progress" (1844), he argues that Christianity's greatest power is the "assimilative" power of the Christ-like character it embodies, and that it is primarily as a vehicle of character that the church carries on the work of Christ in the world. The *Discourses on Christian Nurture* (1847) and the "Argument for 'Discourses on Christian Nurture'" (1847) use this organic model of society to critique the individualistic theory of conversion typical of revivalism. In opposition to the revival, Bushnell affirmed that Christian nurture can and should be a gradual process of growth in which the grace of a Christ-like character is conveyed from parent to passive child through the whole tenor of domestic life. The home, like the church, can organically "assimilate" a person to Christ if only it embodies and expresses the divine form of character that Christ first lived into the world.

Critics of Bushnell's views on Christian nurture frequently asked where the supernatural could possibly figure into this scheme of redemption by education. Thus, the final reading in this section presents Bushnell's case that supernatural energies can and do inhabit the natural channels of human communication. In opposition to the view that miraculous interventions are required to bring the divine into contact with human life in history, Bushnell asserted that the supernatural, once it had entered the stream of the world's life, was available in and through the ordinary structures of experience. In short, as stated in the title of one of his major works, he envisioned *Nature and the Supernatural As Together Constituting the System of God* (1854).

Writings in the second section exemplify Bushnell's use of the social psychology of "Unconscious Influence" to reinterpret the doctrine of the atonement. As one might expect, Bushnell sees Christ accomplishing his redemptive work wholly through the "moral power" of his own perfect character. The end of the work, in turn, is the same as the means; atonement is accomplished through the assimilation of mankind to the divine life, or the communication of Christ-like character. The traditional images associated with the doctrine (e.g. sacrifice, ransom, satisfaction, propitiation) are treated respectfully but secondarily as the "objective" vehicles or "Altar Forms" required for the divine self-expression to have its intended "subjective" effect in the communication of character. Selections here are from Bushnell's major systematic treatments of the atonement: "A Discourse on the Atonement," delivered at Harvard in 1848 and published in *God in Christ;* and *The Vicarious Sacrifice* (1866). A final selection from "Our Gospel a Gift to the Imagination" (1864) shows the close links between Bushnell's doctrine of the atonement and his theory of language.

## NURTURE AND THE SUPERNATURAL
### From "Unconscious Influence" (1846)*

The Bible calls the good man's life a light, and it is the nature of light to flow out spontaneously in all directions, and fill the world unconsciously with its beams. So the Christian shines, it would say, not so much because he will, as because he is a luminous object. Not that the active influence of Christians is made of no account in the figure, but only that this symbol of light has its propriety in the fact that their unconscious influence is the chief influence, and has the precedence in its power over the world. And yet, there are many who will be ready to think that light is a very tame and feeble instrument, because it is noiseless. An earthquake, for example, is to them a much more vigorous and effective agency. Hear how it comes thundering through the solid foundations of nature. It rocks a whole continent. The noblest works of man,—cities, monuments, and temples,—are in a moment leveled to the ground, or swallowed down the opening gulfs of fire. Little do they think that the light of every morning, the soft, and genial, and silent light, is an agent many times more powerful. But let the light of the morning cease and return no more, let the hour of morning come, and bring with it no dawn: the outcries of a horror-stricken world fill the air, and make, as it were, the darkness audible. The beasts go wild and frantic at the loss of the sun. The vegetable growths turn pale and die. A chill creeps on, and frosty winds begin to howl across the freezing earth. Colder, and yet colder, is the night. The vital blood, at length, of all creatures, stops congealed. Down goes the frost toward the earth's center. The heart of the sea is frozen; nay, the earthquakes are themselves frozen in, under their fiery caverns. The very globe itself, too, and all the fellow planets that have lost their sun, are become mere balls of ice, swinging silent in the darkness. Such is the light, which revisits us in the silence of the morning. It makes no shock or scar. It would not wake an infant in his cradle. And yet it perpetually new creates the world, rescuing it, each morning as a prey, from night and chaos. So the Christian is

* [Ed.] First delivered in London. This sermon appears as "Influence of Example" in *American National Preacher*, XX (August 1846), pp. 169–79, and was republished under its present title in *Sermons for the New Life* (New York: Charles Scribner, 1858), pp. 186–205. Included here, from *New Life*: pp. 189–201.

a light, even "the light of the world," and we must not think that, because he shines insensibly or silently, as a mere luminous object, he is therefore powerless. The greatest powers are even those which lie back of the little stirs and commotions of nature; and I verily believe that the insensible influences of good men are as much more potent than what I have called their voluntary or active, as the great silent powers of nature are of greater consequence than her little disturbances and tumults. The law of human influence is deeper than many suspect, and they lose sight of it altogether. The outward endeavors made by good men or bad to sway others, they call their influence; whereas it is, in fact, but a fraction, and, in most cases, but a very small fraction, of the good or evil that flows out of their lives. Nay, I will even go further. How many persons do you meet, the insensible influence of whose manners and character is so decided as often to thwart their voluntary influence; so that, whatever they attempt to do, in the way of controlling others, they are sure to carry the exact opposite of what they intend! And it will generally be found that, where men undertake by argument or persuasion to exert a power, in the face of qualities that make them odious or detestable, or only not entitled to respect, their insensible influence will be too strong for them. The total effect of the life is then of a kind directly opposite to the voluntary endeavor; which, of course, does not add so much as a fraction to it.

I call your attention, next, to the twofold powers of effect and expression by which man connects with his fellow man. If we distinguish man as a creature of language, and thus qualified to communicate himself to others, there are in him two sets or kinds of language, one which is voluntary in the use, and one that is involuntary; that of speech in the literal sense, and that expression of the eye, the face, the look, the gait, the motion, the tone or cadence, which is sometimes called the natural language of the sentiments. This natural language, too, is greatly enlarged by the conduct of life, that which, in business and society, reveals the principles and spirit of men. Speech, or voluntary language, is a door to the soul, that we may open or shut at will; the other is a door that stands open evermore, and reveals to others constantly and often very clearly, the tempers, tastes, and motives of their hearts. Within, as we may represent, is character, charging the common reservoir of influence, and through these twofold gates of the soul, pouring itself out on the world. Out of one it flows at choice, and whensoever we purpose to do good or evil to men. Out of the other it flows each moment, as light from the sun, and propagates itself in all beholders.

Then if we go over to others, that is, to the subjects of influence, we find every man endowed with two inlets of impression; the ear and the understanding for the reception of speech, and the sympathetic powers, the sensibilities or affections, for tinder to those sparks of emotion revealed by looks, tones, manners, and general conduct. And these sympathetic powers, though not immediately rational, are yet inlets, open on all sides, to the understanding and character. They have a certain wonderful capacity to receive impressions, and catch the meaning of signs, and propagate in us whatsoever falls into their passive molds, from others. The impressions they receive do not come through verbal propositions, and are never received into verbal proposition, it may be, in the mind, and therefore many think nothing of them. But precisely on this account are they the more powerful, because it is as if one heart were thus going directly into another, and carrying in its feelings with it. Beholding, as in a glass, the feelings of our neighbor, we are changed into the same image, by the assimilating power of sensibility and fellow-feeling.* Many have gone so far, and not without show, at least, of reason, as to maintain that the look or expression, and even the very features of children, are often changed, by exclusive intercourse with nurses and attendants. Furthermore, if we carefully consider, we shall find it scarcely possible to doubt, that simply to look on bad and malignant faces, or those whose expressions have become infected by vice, to be with them and become familiarized to them, is enough permanently to affect the character of persons of mature age. I do not say that it must of necessity subvert their character, for the evil looked upon may never be loved or welcomed in practice; but it is something to have these bad images in the soul, giving out their expressions there, and diffusing their odor among the thoughts, as long as we live. How dangerous a thing is it, for example, for a man to become accustomed to sights of cruelty? What man, valuing the honor of his soul, would not shrink from yielding himself to such an influence? No more is it a thing of indifference to become accustomed to look on the manners, and receive the bad expression of any kind of sin.

The door of involuntary communication, I have said, is always open. Of course we are communicating ourselves in this way to others, at every moment of our intercourse or presence with them. But how very seldom, in comparison, do we undertake by means of speech to influence others! Even the best Christian, one who most improves his opportunities to do good, attempts but seldom to sway another by voluntary influence, whereas he is all the while shining as a luminous object unawares, and communicating of his heart to the world.

But there is yet another view of this double line of communication which man has with his fellow-men, which is more general, and displays the import of the truth yet more convincingly. It is by one of these modes of communication that we are constituted members of voluntary

---

* [Ed.] The sentence transposes II Corinthians 3:18 into the terms of Bushnell's social psychology.

society, and by the other, parts of a general mass, or members of involuntary society. You are all, in a certain view, individuals, and separate as
persons from each other: you are also, in a certain other view, parts of a
common body, as truly as the parts of a stone. Thus if you ask how it is
that you and all men came, without your consent, to exist in society, to
be within its power, to be under its laws, the answer is, that while you
are a man, you are also a fractional element of a larger and more comprehensive being, called society—be it the family, the church, the state.
In a certain department of your nature, it is open; its sympathies and
feelings are open. On this open side you all adhere together, as parts of a
larger nature, in which there is a common circulation of want, impulse,
and law. Being thus made common to each other unwittingly, you
become one mass, one consolidated social body, animated by one life.
And observe how far this involuntary communication and sympathy
between the members of a state or family is sovereign over their character. It always results in what we call the national or family spirit; for
there is a spirit peculiar to every state and family in the world. Sometimes, too, this national or family spirit takes a religious or an irreligious
character, and appears almost to absorb the religious self-government of
individuals. What was the national spirit of France, for example, at a
certain time, but a spirit of infidelity? What is the religious spirit of
Spain at this moment, but a spirit of bigotry, quite as wide of Christianity and destructive to character as the spirit of falsehood? What is the
family spirit in many a house, but the spirit of gain, or pleasure, or
appetite, in which every thing that is warm, dignified, genial, and good
in religion, is visibly absent? Sometimes you will almost fancy that you
see the shapes of money in the eyes of the children. So it is that we are
led on by nations, as it were, to a good or bad immortality. Far down in
the secret foundations of life and society, there lie concealed great laws
and channels of influence, which make the race common to each other
in all the main departments or divisions of the social mass—laws which
often escape our notice altogether, but which are to society as gravity to
the general system of God's works.

But these are general considerations, and more fit, perhaps, to give
you a rational conception of the modes of influence and their relative
power, than to verify that conception, or establish its truth. I now proceed to add, therefore, some miscellaneous proofs of a more particular
nature.

And I mention, first of all, the instinct of imitation in children. We
begin our moral experience, not with acts grounded in judgment or
reason, or with ideas received through language, but by simple imitation,
and, under the guidance of this, we lay our foundations. The child looks
and listens, and whatsoever tone of feeling or manner of conduct is displayed around him, sinks into his plastic, passive soul, and becomes a

mold of his being ever after. The very handling of the nursery is significant, and the petulance, the passion, the gentleness, the tranquillity indi-
cated by it, are all reproduced in the child. His soul is a purely receptive
nature, and that, for a considerable period, without choice or selection. A
little further on, he begins voluntarily to copy every thing he sees. Voice,
manner, gait, every thing which the eye sees, the mimic instinct delights
to act over. And thus we have a whole generation of future men, receiving from us their very beginnings, and the deepest impulses of their life
and immortality. They watch us every moment, in the family, before the
hearth, and at the table; and when we are meaning them no good or
evil, when we are conscious of exerting no influence over them, they are
drawing from us impressions and molds of habit, which, if wrong, no
heavenly discipline can wholly remove; or, if right, no bad associations
utterly dissipate. Now it may be doubted, I think, whether, in all the
active influence of our lives, we do as much to shape the destiny of our
fellow-men, as we do in this single article of unconscious influence over
children. . . .

Is it also true, you may ask, that the religious spirit propagates itself
or tends to propagate itself in the same way? I see no reason to question
that it does. Nor does any thing in the doctrine of spiritual influences,
when rightly understood, forbid the supposition. For spiritual influences
are never separated from the laws of thought in the individual, and the
laws of feeling and influence in society. If, too, every disciple is to be an
"epistle known and read of all men,"* what shall we expect, but that all
men will be somehow affected by the reading? Or, if he is to be a light
in the world, what shall we look for, but that others, seeing his good
works, shall glorify God on his account? How often is it seen too as a fact
of observation, that one, or a few good men kindle at length a holy fire
in the community in which they live, and become the leaven of a general reformation! Such men give a more vivid proof in their persons of
the reality of religious faith, than any words or arguments could yield.
They are active; they endeavor, of course, to exert a good voluntary
influence; but still their chief power lies in their holiness, and the sense
they produce in others of their close relation to God. . . .

And here I must conduct you to a yet higher example, even that of
the Son of God, the light of the world. Men dislike to be swayed by
direct, voluntary influence. They are jealous of such control, and are
therefore best approached by conduct and feeling, and the authority of
simple worth, which seem to make no purposed onset. If goodness
appears, they welcome its celestial smile; if heaven descends to encircle
them, they yield to its sweetness; if truth appears in the life, they honor
it with a secret homage; if personal majesty and glory appear, they bow

* [Ed.] Viz. II Corinthians 3:2.

with reverence, and acknowledge with shame, their own vileness. Now it is on this side of human nature that Christ visits us, preparing just that kind of influence which the spirit of truth may wield with the most persuasive and subduing effect. It is the grandeur of his character which constitutes the chief power of his ministry, not his miracles or teachings apart from his character. Miracles were useful, at the time, to arrest attention, and his doctrine is useful at all times as the highest revelation of truth possible in speech; but the greatest truth of the gospel, notwithstanding, is Christ himself—a human body become the organ of the divine nature, and revealing, under the conditions of an earthly life, the glory of God! The Scripture writers have much to say, in this connection, of the image of God: and an image, you know, is that which simply represents, not that which acts, or reasons, or persuades. Now it is this image of God which makes the center, the sun itself, of the gospel. The journeyings, teachings, miracles, and sufferings of Christ, all had their use in bringing out this image, or what is the same, in making conspicuous the character and feelings of God, both toward sinners and toward sin. And here is the power of Christ—it is what of God's beauty, love, truth, and justice shines through him. It is the influence which flows unconsciously and spontaneously out of Christ, as the friend of man, the light of the world, the glory of the Father, made visible. And some have gone so far as to conjecture that God made the human person, originally, with a view to its becoming the organ or vehicle, by which he might reveal his communicable attributes to other worlds. Christ, they believe, came to inhabit this organ, that he might execute a purpose so sublime. The human person is constituted, they say, to be a mirror of God; and God, being imaged in that mirror, as in Christ, is held up to the view of this and other worlds. It certainly is to the view of this; and if the Divine nature can use this organ so effectively to express itself unto us, if it can bring itself, through the looks, tones, motions, and conduct of a human person, more close to our sympathies than by any other means, how can we think that an organ so communicative, inhabited by us, is not always breathing our spirit and transferring our image insensibly to others?

# From "Growth Not Conquest
the True Method of Christian Progress" (1844)*

[C]onsider the whole discipline of a Christian life, as a perpetual exercise in character. . . . And how great a power is character! Out of God's own person and his truth, there is no other so mighty and persuasive. It is that eloquence which man least knows how to resist. It provokes no resistance. Being itself only truth in life, it suffers no answer. If the beholder turns away to escape the homage he feels, its image still goes with him, to reprove his evil deeds and call him every hour to God. . . .

The church, in like manner, is to the world's eye a development of God. Being the body of Christ, she is, in some sense, though not in the sense of Mr. Brownson and the Papists,† a perpetual Christ in the earth—in the sense, we mean, not of her political organization, but of her practical or internal spirit. By this she becomes the light of the world, as her Savior was—a perpetual manifestation of the Spirit, or what is the same, of the Divine Nature. This too is the main source of her power over the world. It is not because she runs to and fro, because she strives and cries, but because she lives a life above nature,—herein lies her capacity of impression. Without saying, "this is God," the world is moved as by the presence and power of God. Her Christ-like graces of love, purity, truth, and beneficence, are a divine atmosphere about her, and her atmosphere enters the breath and blood, while her arguments only play about the head. To approach her is to be convinced of sin, righteousness, and judgement to come. To be thus, in her Christian growth, a demonstration of the Spirit, to have the divine nature flowing out thus inpalpably but really on the world, gives her an *assimilative power* in the nature of vitality. So that if she gains a convert, whether at

---

* [Ed.] First published as "The Kingdom of Heaven as a Grain of Mustard Seed," *The New Englander*, II (October 1844), pp. 600–619. Republished under the present title in *Views of Christian Nurture* (Hartford: Edwin Hunt, 1847), pp. 147–81. Included here, from *Views*: pp. 170–73, 178–79.

† [Ed.] Orestes Augustus Brownson (1803–1876) passed through several varieties of religious liberalism on his way to a final berth in Roman Catholicism in 1844 (the year of Bushnell's paper).

home or in the ends of the earth, (for place is nothing,) it is not by external conquest but by virtue of her own internal life—the life of God. . . .

One principal reason why we are so often deficient in character, or
outward beauty, is, that piety begins so late in life, having thus to maintain a perpetual and unequal war with previous habit. If it was not true
of Paul, it is yet too generally true, that one born out of due time will be
found out of due time, more often than he should be afterwards—
unequal, inconsistent with himself, acting the old man instead of the
new. Having the old habit to war with, it is often too strong for him. To
make a graceful and complete Christian character, it needs itself to be
the habit of existence;—not a grape grafted on a bramble. And this, it
will be seen, requires a Christian childhood in the subject. Having this,
the gracious or supernatural character becomes itself more nearly natural, and possesses the peculiar charm of naturalness, which is necessary
to the highest moral beauty.

It results also from our mistaken views of Christian training, that we
fall into a notion of religion that is mechanical. . . . Our only idea of
increase is of that which accrues by means of a certain abrupt technical
experience. Led away thus from all thought of internal growth in the
church, efforts to secure conversions take an external character, which is
not proper to them. Accretion displaces growth. The church is gathered
as a foundling hospital, and lest it should not be so, its own children are
reduced to foundlings. Immediate repentance proclaimed, insisted on
and realized in an abrupt change, proper only to those who are indeed
aliens and enemies, is the only hope or inlet of the church. We can not
understand how the spiritual nation should grow and populate and
become powerful within itself;—nothing will serve but the immediate
annexation of Texas!

Piety becomes inconstant, and revivals of religion take an exagger-
ated character from the same causes. If all Christian success is measured
by the count of technical conversions from without, then it follows that
nothing is done when conversions cease to be counted. The harvest closes
not with feasting but with famine. Despair cuts off Christian motive.
The tide is spent, let us anchor during the ebb. It is well indeed to live
very piously in the families, still there is nothing depending on it. The
children will be good subjects enough for conversion without. The piety
of the church is thus made to be desultory and irregular by system. The
idea of conquest displaces the idea of growth. Whereas, if it were understood that Christian education, or training in the families, is to be itself a
process of domestic conversion, that as a child weeps under a frown and
smiles at the command of a smile, so spiritual influences may be streaming into his being from the handling of the nursery and the whole manner and temperament of the house, producing what will ever after be
fundamental impressions of his being; then the hearth, the table, the

society and affections of the house, would all feel the presence of a practical religious motive. The homes would be Christian homes, and life itself a stream of genial piety. . . .

From *Views of Christian Nurture*,
"An Argument for
'Discourses on Christian Nurture'" (1847)*

[The piety of revivalism makes for] a religion that begins explosively, raises high frames, carries little or no expansion, and after the day is spent, subsides into a torpor. Considered as a distinct era, introduced by Edwards, and extended and caricatured by his contemporaries, it has one great merit and one great defect. The merit is, that it displaced an era of dead formality, and brought in the demand of a truly spiritual and supernatural experience. The defect is, that it has cast a type of religious individualism, intense beyond any former example. It makes nothing of the family, and the church, and the organic powers God has constituted as vehicles of grace. It takes every man as if he had existed *alone*, presumes that he is unreconciled to God until he has undergone some sudden and explosive experience, in adult years, or after the age of reason; demands that experience, and only when it is reached, allows the subject to be an heir of life. Then, on the other side, or that of the Spirit of God, the very act or *ictus* by which the change is wrought, is isolated or individualized, so as to stand in no connexion with any other of God's means or causes—an epiphany, in which God leaps from the stars, or some place above, to do a work apart from all system, or connection with his other works. Religion is thus a kind of transcendental matter, which belongs on the outside of life, and has no part in the laws by which life is organized—a miraculous epidemic, a fireball shot from the moon, something holy because it is from God, but so extraordinary, so out of place, that it cannot suffer any vital connexion with the ties and causes and forms and habits, which constitute the frame of our history. Hence the desultory, hard, violent and often extravagant or erratic character it manifests. Hence, in part, the dreary years of decay and darkness, that interspace our months of excitement and victory.

* [Ed.] *Views of Christian Nurture* (Hartford: Edwin Hunt, 1847) pp. 49–121. Included here: pp. 68–69.

# From *Discourses on Christian Nurture* (1847)*

What is the true idea of Christian education?—I answer in the following proposition, which it will be the aim of my argument to establish, viz:

THAT THE CHILD IS TO GROW UP A CHRISTIAN. In other words, the aim, effort and expectation should be, not, as is commonly assumed, that the child is to grow up in sin, to be converted after he comes to a mature age; but that he is to open on the world as one that is spiritually renewed, not remembering the time when he went through a technical experience, but seeming rather to have loved what is good from his earliest years. . . .

We are to understand, that a right spirit may be virtually exercised in children, when, as yet, it is not intellectually received, or as a form of doctrine. Thus if they are put upon an effort to be good, connecting the fact that God desires it and will help them in the endeavor, that is all which, in a very early age, they can receive, and that includes every thing—repentance, love, duty, dependence, faith. Nay, the operative truth necessary to a new life, may possibly be communicated through and from the parent, being revealed in his looks, manners and ways of life, before they are of an age to understand the teachings of words; for the Christian scheme, the gospel, is really wrapped up in the life of every Christian parent and beams out from him as a living epistle, before it escapes from the lips, or is taught in words. And the Spirit of truth may as well make this living truth effectual, as the preaching of the gospel itself. Never is it too early for good to be communicated. Infancy and childhood are the ages most pliant to good. And who can think it necessary that the plastic nature of childhood must first be hardened into stone, and stiffened into enmity towards God and all duty, before it can become a candidate for Christian character! There could not be a more unnecessary mistake, and it is as unnatural and pernicious, I fear, as it is unnecessary.

There are many who assume the radical goodness of human nature, and the work of Christian education is, in their view, only to educate, or educe the good that is in us. Let no one be disturbed by the suspicion of a

* [Ed.] Originally published in pamphlet form by the Massachusetts Sabbath School Society (Boston: 1847). Republished in *Views of Christian Nurture* (Hartford: Edwin Hunt, 1847), pp. 5–47. Included here, from *Views*: pp. 6, 14–22.

coincidence between what I have here said and such a theory. The natural pravity of man is plainly asserted in the scriptures, and, if it were not, the familiar laws of physiology would require us to believe, what amounts to the same thing. And if neither scripture nor physiology taught us the doctrine, if the child was born as clear of natural prejudice or damage, as Adam before his sin, spiritual education, or, what is the same, probation, that which trains a being for a stable, intelligent virtue hereafter, would still involve an experiment of evil, therefore a fall and bondage under the laws of evil; so that, view the matter as we will, there is no so unreasonable assumption, none so wide of all just philosophy, as that which proposes to form a child to virtue, by simply educing or drawing out what is in him. The growth of Christian virtue is no vegetable process, no mere onward development. It involves a struggle with evil, a fall and rescue. The soul becomes established in holy virtue, as a free exercise, only as it is passed round the corner of fall and redemption, ascending thus unto God through a double experience, in which it learns the bitterness of evil and the worth of good, fighting its way out of one and achieving the other as a victory. The child, therefore, may as well begin life under a law of hereditary damage, as to plunge himself into evil by his own experiment, which he will as naturally do from the simple impulse of curiosity, or the instinct of knowledge, as from any noxious quality in his mold derived by descent. For it is not sin which he derives from his parents; at least not sin in any sense which imports blame, but only some prejudice to the perfect harmony of his mold, some kind of pravity or obliquity which inclines him to evil. These suggestions are offered, not as necessary to be received in every particular, but simply to show that the scheme of education proposed, is not to be identified with another, which assumes the radical goodness of human nature, and according to which, if it be true, Christian education is insignificant. . . .

Once more, if we narrowly examine the relation of parent and child, we shall not fail to discover something like a law of organic connection,* as regards character, subsisting between them. Such a connection as makes it easy to believe, and natural to expect that the faith of the one

* Some persons have blamed the use here made of the term "organic", as a singularity of mine. So far from that, it is a term in common philosophic use in connection with all the great questions of government and society. The days of the "social compact" theory, for example, are gone by, and it is now held by almost all the late writers, that we naturally exist as organic bodies, just as we do as individuals, and that civil government is born with us, in virtue of our organic unity in bodies or States—that the State must legislate for itself in some way, just as the conscience legislates for the individual. Government is, in this view, the organic conscience of the State—no matter what may be the form, or who presides. ([Ed.] Bushnell here may have had in mind the social theory put forward by Edmund Burke in *Reflections on the Revolution in France* [1790], or by Samuel Taylor Coleridge in *On the Constitution of the Church and State* [1830].)

will be propagated in the other. Perhaps I should rather say, such a connection as induces the conviction that the character of one is actually included in that of the other, as a seed is formed in the capsule; and being there matured, by a nutriment derived from the stem, is gradually separated from it. It is a singular fact, that many believe substantially the same thing, in regard to evil character, but have no thought of any such possibility in regard to good. There has been much speculation, of late, as to whether a child is born in depravity, or whether the depraved character is superinduced afterwards. But, like many other great questions, it determines much less than is commonly supposed; for, according to the most proper view of the subject, a child is really not born till he emerges from the infantile state, and never before that time can be said to receive a separate and properly individual nature. The declaration of scripture, and the laws of physiology, I have already intimated, compel the belief that a child's nature is somehow depraved by descent from parents, who are under the corrupting effects of sin. But this, taken as a question relating to the mere *punctum temporis*, or precise point of birth, is not a question of any so grave import, as is generally supposed; for the child, after birth, is still within the matrix of the parental life, and will be more or less, for many years. And the parental life will be flowing into him all that time, just as naturally, and by a law as truly organic, as when the sap of the trunk flows into a limb. We must not govern our thoughts, in such a matter, by our eyes; and because the physical separation has taken place, conclude that no organic relation remains. Even the physical being of the child is dependent still for nutrition on organic processes not in itself. Meantime, the mental being and character have scarcely begun to have a proper individual life. Will, in connection with conscience, is the basis of personality, or individuality, and these exist as yet only in their rudimental type, as when the form of a seed is beginning to be unfolded at the root of a flower. At first, the child is held as a mere passive lump in the arms, and he opens into conscious life under the soul of the parent streaming into his eyes and ears, through the manners and tones of the nursery. The kind and degree of passivity are gradually changed as life advances. A little farther on it is observed that a smile wakens a smile—any kind of sentiment or passion, playing in the face of the parent, wakens a responsive sentiment or passion. Irritation irritates, a frown wither's, love expands a look congenial to itself, and why not holy love? Next the ear is opened to the understanding of words, but what words the child shall hear, he cannot choose, and has as little capacity to select the sentiments that are poured into his soul. Farther on, the parents begin to govern him by appeals to will, expressed in commands, and whatever their requirement may be, he can as little withstand it, as the violet can cool the scorching sun, or the tattered leaf can tame the hurricane. Next they appoint his school, choose his books, regulate his company, decide what form of religion, and what religious opinions he shall be taught, by taking him to a church of their own selection. In all this, they infringe upon no right of the child, they only fulfill an office which belongs to them. Their will and character are designed to be the matrix of the child's will and character. Meantime he approaches more and more closely, and by a gradual process, to the proper rank and responsibility of an individual creature, during all which process of separation, he is having their exercises and ways translated into him. Then, at last, he comes forth to act his part in such color of evil, (and why not of good?) as he has derived from them. The tendency of all our modern speculations is to an extreme individualism, and we carry our doctrines of free will so far as to make little or nothing of organic laws; not observing that character may be, to a great extent, only the free development of exercises previously wrought in us, or extended to us, when other wills had us within their sphere. . . .

And this is the very idea of Christian education, that it begins with nurture or cultivation. And the intention is that the Christian life and spirit of the parents shall flow into the mind of the child, to blend with his incipient and half-formed exercises; that they shall thus beget their own good within him, their thoughts, opinions, faith and love, which are to become a little more, and yet a little more, his own separate exercise, but still the same in character. The contrary assumption, that virtue must be the product of separate and absolutely independent choice, is pure assumption. As regards the measure of personal merit and demerit, it is doubtless true that every subject of God is to be responsible only for what is his own. But virtue still is rather a *state* of being than an act or series of acts; and if we look at the causes which induce or prepare such a state, the will of the person himself may have a part among those causes more or less important, and it works no absurdity to suppose that one may be even prepared to such a state, by causes prior to his own will; so that, when he sets off to act for himself, his struggle and duty may be rather to sustain and perfect the state begun, than to produce a new one. Certain it is that we are never, at any age, so independent as to be wholly out of the reach of organic laws which affect our character. All society is organic—the church, the state, the school, the family,—and there is a spirit in each of these organisms, peculiar to itself, and more or less hostile, more or less favorable, to religious character, and to some extent, at least, sovereign over the individual man. A very great share of the power in what is called a revival of religion, is organic power; nor is it any the less divine on that account. The child is only more within the power of organic laws than we all are. We possess only a mixed individuality all our life long. A pure, separate, individual man, living *wholly* within, and from himself, is a mere fiction. No such person ever existed, or ever can. I need not say that this view of an organic connection of character subsisting between parent and child, lays a basis for notions of Christian education, far different from those which now prevail, under the cover of a merely fictitious and mischievous individualism.

Perhaps it may be necessary to add, that, in the strong language I have used concerning the organic connection of character between the parent and the child, it is not designed to assert a power in the parent to renew the child, or that the child can be renewed by any agency of the Spirit less immediate, than that which renews the parent himself. When a germ is formed on the stem of any plant, the formative instinct of the plant may be said in one view to produce it; but the same solar heat which quickens the plant, must quicken also the germ and sustain the internal action of growth, by a common presence in both. So if there be an organic power of character in the parent, such as that of which I have spoken, it is not a complete power in itself, but only such a power as demands the realizing presence of the Spirit of God, both in the parent and the child, to give it effect. As Paul said, "I have begotten you through the gospel,"* so may we say of the parent, who having a living gospel enveloped in his life, brings it into organic connection with the soul of childhood. But the declaration excludes the necessity of a divine influence, not more in one case than in the other.

* [Ed.] I Corinthians 4:15.

# From *Views of Christian Nurture,*
## "An Argument for
## 'Discourses on Christian Nurture'" (1847)*

[T]here are two modes of viewing this whole subject [of Christian nurture], both equally correct, but not equally apposite to my particular purposes. And the two have about the same relation to each other that the rainbow, as a positive institution, has to the rainbow, as a product of the world's laws. If I take my position by the covenant of Abraham† and hang my doctrine of nurture on that, as a positive institution, or, what is the same, on its promises; if then I contemplate God as coming in by his spirit from a point of isolation above, in answer to prayer, or without, to work in the child's heart, whether by a divine stroke or *ictus* apart from all connexion of cause and consequence or not, the change called regeneration, and thus to fulfill the promise; I realize indeed a form of unquestionable supernaturalism. . . . [But] just as the reality of the rainbow is in the world's laws prior to the covenant with Noah, so there is, in the organic laws of the race, a reality or ground answering to the covenant with Abraham; only, in this latter case, the reality is a supernatural grace which inhabits the organic laws of nature and works its results in conformity with them. . . .

If I handled my subject wholly within the first form, or under the type of the covenant as a positive institution, I presume I should have found a much readier assent, and that for the very reason that I had thrown my grounds of expectation for Christian nurture the other side of the fixed stars, whereby the parent himself is delivered from all connexion with the results, and from all responsibility concerning them. He will reverently acknowledge that he has imparted a mold of depravity, but the laws of connexion between him and his child are operative, he thinks, only for this bad purpose. If any good comes to the child, it must

---

* [Ed.] *Views of Christian Nurture* (Hartford: Edwin Hunt, 1847) pp. 49–121. Included here: pp. 99–100.
† [Ed.] Bushnell here refers to Genesis 17:7, in which God promises to "be a God" to Abraham and his "seed." In orthodox Puritan theology, this text grounded the doctrine of the "household covenant," assuring Christian parents that their children were highly likely to receive the grace of conversion when they came of age. Bushnell frequently claimed that his own theory of nurture simply described the social-psychological mechanism of the connection between parents and children affirmed by the "household covenant."

come straight down from the island occupied by Jehovah, to the child as an individual, and does not, in its coming, take the organic laws of parental character on its way to regenerate and sanctify them as its vehicle. As regards a remedy for individualism, little is gained, even if the doctrine that children ought to be trained up in the way they should go is believed; for there is no effectual or sufficient remedy, *till the laws of grace are seen to be perfectly coincident with the organic laws of depravity.* Therefore it was necessary to keep to the naturalistic form. But I meant to interpose all the safeguards necessary to save myself from proper naturalism, and I supposed that I had done it.*

* [Ed.] In fact, Bushnell was not yet satisfied that he had "done it." His continuing concern with the distinction and interrelations of nature and the supernatural resulted in another book; *Nature and the Supernatural*, (New York: Charles Scribner, 1858), which is excerpted below.

# From *Nature and the Supernatural* (1858)*

In order to the intelligent prosecution of our subject, we need, first of all, to settle on the true import of certain words and phrases by the undistinguishing and confused use of which, more than by any other cause, the unbelieving habit of our time has been silently and imperceptibly determined. They are such as these:—"nature," "the system of nature," "the laws of nature," "universal nature," "the supernatural," and the like. The first and last named, "nature" and the "supernatural," most need our attention; for, if these are carefully distinguished, the others will scarcely fail to yield us their true meaning.

The Latin etymology of the word *nature*, presents the true force of the term, clear of all ambiguity. The nature [*natura*] of a thing is the future particle of its being or becoming—its *about-to-be*, or its *about-to-come-to-pass*,—and the radical idea is, that there is, in the thing whose nature we speak of, or in the whole of things called nature, an about-to-be, a definite futurition, a fixed law of coming to pass, such that, given the thing, or whole of things, all the rest will follow by an inherent necessity. In this view, nature, sometimes called "universal nature," and sometimes "the system of nature," is that created realm of being or substance which has an acting, a going on or process from within itself, under and by its own laws. Or, if we say, with some, that the laws are but another name for the immediate actuating power of God, still it makes no difference, in any other respect, with our conception of the system. It is yet *as if* the laws, the powers, the actings, were inherent in the substances, and were by them determined. It is still to our scientific separated from our religious contemplation, a chain of causes and effects, or a scheme or orderly succession, determined from within the scheme itself.

Having settled, thus, our conception of nature, our conception of the supernatural corresponds. That is supernatural, whatever it be, that is either not in the chain of natural cause and effect, or which acts on the chain of cause and effect, in nature, from without the chain. Thus if any event transpires in the bosom, or upon the platform of what is called nature, which is not from nature itself, or is varied from the process

* [Ed.] *Nature and the Supernatural, As Together Constituting the One System of God* (New York: Charles Scribner, 1858). Included here: pp. 36–37, 42–44, 84–86, 98–102.

nature would execute by her own laws, that is supernatural, by whatever power it is wrought. . . . So, if the processes, combinations, and results of our system of nature are interrupted, or varied by the action, whether of God, or angels, or men, so as to bring to pass what would not come to pass in it by its own internal action, under the laws of mere cause and effect, the variations are, in like manner, supernatural.* And exactly this we expect to show: viz., that God has, in fact, erected another and higher system, that of spiritual being and government, for which nature exists; a system not under the law of cause and effect, but ruled and marshaled under other kinds of laws and able continually to act upon, or vary the action of the processes of nature. If, accordingly, we speak of system, this spiritual realm or department is much more properly called a system than the natural, because it is closer to God, higher in its consequence, and contains in itself the ends, or final causes, for which the other exists and to which the other is made to be subservient. There is, however, a constant action and reaction between the two, and, strictly speaking, they are both together, taken as one, the true system of God. . . .

That what we have defined as nature truly exists will not be doubted, but that there is any being or power in the universe, who acts, or can act upon the chain of cause and effect in nature from without the chain, many will doubt and some will strenuously deny. Indeed the great difficulty heretofore encountered, in establishing the faith of a supernatural agency, has been due to the fact that we have made a ghost of it; discussing it as if it were a marvel of superstition, and no definite and credible reality. Whereas, it will appear, as we confront our difficulty more thoughtfully and take its full force, that the moment we begin to conceive ourselves rightly, we become ourselves supernatural. It is no longer necessary to go hunting after marvels, apparitions, suspensions of the laws of nature, to find the supernatural; it meets us in what is least transcendent and most familiar, even in ourselves. In ourselves we discover a tier of existences that are above nature and, in all their most ordinary actions, are doing their will upon it. The very idea of our personality is that of a being not under the law of cause and effect, a being supernatural. This one point clearly apprehended, all the difficulties of our subject are at once relieved, if not absolutely and completely removed.

If any one is startled or shocked by what appears to be the extravagance of this position, let him recur to our definition; viz., that nature is that world of substance, whose laws are laws of cause and effect, and

---

* [Ed.] Bushnell's definitions of nature and the supernatural are borrowed directly from Coleridge's *Aids to Reflection*. Compare the above passages with the *Aids* (1840; rpt. Port Washington, N.Y.: Kennikat Press, 1971), pp. 108n, 110, and 236.

whose events transpire, in orderly succession, under those laws; the supernatural is that range of substance, if any such there be, that acts upon the chain of cause and effect in nature from without the chain, producing, thus, results that, by mere nature, could not come to pass. It is not said, be it observed, as is sometimes done, that the supernatural implies a suspension of the laws of nature, a causing them, for the time, not to be—that, perhaps, is never done—it is only said that we, as powers, not in the line of cause and effect, can set the causes in nature at work, in new combinations otherwise never occurring, and produce, by our action upon nature, results which she, as nature, could never produce by her own internal acting.

Illustrations are at hand without number. Thus, nature, for example, never made a pistol, or gunpowder, or pulled a trigger; all which being done, or procured to be done, by the criminal, in his act of murder, he is hung for what is rightly called his unnatural deed. So of things not criminal; nature never built a house, or modeled a ship, or fitted a coat, or invented a steam-engine, or wrote a book, or framed a constitution. These are all events that spring out of human liberty, acting in and upon the realm of cause and effect, to produce results and combinations, which mere cause and effect could not; and, at some point of the process in each, we shall be found coming down upon nature, by an act of sovereignty just as peremptory and mysterious as that which is discovered in a miracle, only that a miracle is a similar coming down upon it from another and higher being, and not from ourselves. . . .

[Thus] we do positively know existences that can not be included in nature, but constitute a higher range, empowered to act upon it. This higher range we are ourselves, as already shown by our definition of nature and the supernatural in the last chapter. By that definition we are now prepared to assume and formally assign the grand twofold distinction of *things* and *persons*, or *things* and *powers*. All free intelligences, it was shown, the created and the uncreated, are, as being free, essentially supernatural in their action; having all, in the matter of their will, a power transcending cause and effect in nature, by which they are able to act on the lines and vary the combinations of natural causalities. They differ, in short, from every thing that classes under the term nature, in the fact that they act from themselves, uncaused in their action. They are powers, not things; the radical idea of a power being that of an agent, or force, which acts from itself, uncaused, initiating trains of effect that flow from itself.

Of the two great classes, therefore, named in our distribution, one comprehends all beings that are able to originate new trains of effects,— these are the Powers; and the other is made up of such as can only propagate effects under certain fixed laws,—these are Things. At the head of one class we conceive is God, as Lord of Hosts; who, in virtue of his all-originating power as Creator, is called the First Cause; having round him innumerable orders of intelligence which, though caused to exist by Him, are as truly first causes in their action as He,—starting all their trains of consequences in the same manner. In the other class, we have the immense catalogue of what are called the natural sciences,—the astronomical bodies, the immaterial forces, the fluids and solids of the world, the elements and atoms of chemistry, the dynamics of life and instinct,—in all of which, what are called causes are only propagations of effects under and by fixed laws. Hence they are second causes only; that is, causes whose causations are determined by others back of them; never, in any sense, originative, or first causes. The completeness of the distribution will be yet more clear, and the immense abyss of distance between the two orders, or classes, more visibly impassable, if we add such points of contrast as the following:—

Powers, acting in liberty, are capable of a double action,—to do, or not to do, (God, for example, in creating, man in sinning;) things can act only in one way, viz; as their law determines.

Powers are perfectible only by exercise, after they are made; things are perfect as made.

Powers are perfected, or established in their law, only by a schooling of their consent; things are under a law mechanical at the first, having no consent.

Powers can violate the present or nearest harmony, moving disorder in it; things are incapable of disorder, save as they are disordered by the malign action of powers.

Powers, governed by the absolute force or fiat of onmipotence, would in that fact be uncreated and cease; things exist and act only in and by the impulsion of that fiat.

We have thus drawn out and set before us two distinct orders and degrees of being, which, together, constitute the real universe. So perfectly diverse are they in kind, that no common terms of law or principle can, for one moment, be imagined to include them both; they can be one system only in some higher and broader sense, which subordinates one to the other, or both to the same final causes. One thing is thus made clear; viz., that nature is not, in any proper sense, the universe. We know that it is not, because we find another kind of existence in ourselves, which consciously does not fall within the terms of nature. . . .

If now we raise the question more distinctly, what is the great problem of existence, as regards the order of powers, or the human race as being such, it is not difficult to answer, following out the view thus far presented, that it is our perfection; the perfection, that is, of our liberty, the schooling of our choice, or consent, as powers, so that we may be fully established in harmony with God's will and character; unified with Him in his will, glorified with Him in the glory of his character, and so perfected with Him in his eternal beatitude. Persons or powers are creatures, we have seen, who act, not by causality, but by consent; they must, therefore, be set in conditions that invite consent, and treated also in a manner that permits the caprices of liberty. It is also a remarkable distinction, we have noted, that they are creatures perfectible only after they are made, while mere natural quantities and objects are perfect as made. Just here, accordingly, the grand problem of their life and of the world begins. They are to be trained, formed, furnished, perfected; and to this end are to be carried through just such scenes, experiences, changes, trials, variations, operations, as will best serve their spiritual perfection and their final fruition of each other and of God. If there are necessary perils in such a trial of their liberty, then they are to be set upon the course of such perils. Nor will it make any difference if the perils are such as breed the greatest speculative difficulties. God does not frame his empire to suit and satisfy our speculations, but for our practical profit; to bring us up into His own excellence, and establish us eternally in the participation of his character. On this subject there would seem to be very little room for doubt. The scripture revelation proposes this view of life, our own observation confirms it, and besides there is really no other in which even our philosophy can comfortably rest.

But this training of consent, this perfecting of liberty in the issues of character, it will help us at this early point to observe, is nothing different from a preparation for society and a drill-practice in the principles of society; that is, in truth, in purity, in justice, in patience, forgiveness, love, all the self-renouncing and beneficent virtues. Accordingly the course of training will itself be social; a trial under, in, and by society. The powers will be thrown together in terms of duty as being terms of society, and in terms of society as being terms of duty. Morality and the law of religion respect society and the condition of social well-being, which is the grand felicity of powers. Things have no society, or capacity of social relations. In mere nature, considered as a scheme of cause and effect, there is nothing social, any more than there is in the members of a steam-engine. And if we really believe that we ourselves are only wheels, in the play of an all-comprehending causation, it should be the end even of the feeling of society in us. Love, benefit, sympathy, injury, hatred, thanks, blame, character, worship, faith,—all that constitutes the reality of society, whether of men with God or of men with each other, belongs to the fact that we are consciously powers. Strip us of this, let all these fruits be regarded as mere dynamic results, under the head of natural philosophy, and they will change, at once, to be mere tricks, or impostures of natural magic. Our discipline, therefore, is to be such as our supernatural and social quality requires, the discipline of society.

Since it is for society, it must be in and by society. We accordingly shall have a training as powers among other powers, such as will qualify us for a place of eternal unity and harmony with them under God, the central and First Power; so to be set by Him in a consolidated, everlasting kingdom of righteousness, and truth, and love, and peace.

And thus it is that we find ourselves embodied in matter, to act as powers upon, for, with, and, if we will, against each other, in all the endless complications of look, word, act, art, force, and persuasion; in the family and in the state, or two and two upon each other; in marriage, fraternity, neighborhood, friendship, trade, association, protection, hospitality, instruction, sympathy; or, if we will, in frauds, enmities, oppressions, cruelties, and mutual temptations,—great men moving the age they live in by their eloquence; or shaping the ages to come by their institutions; or corrupting the world's moral atmosphere by their bad thoughts, their fashions and vices; or tearing and desolating all things by irruptions of war, to win a throne of empire, or the honors of victors and heroes. By all these methods do we come into society, and begin to act, each one, upon the trains of cause and effect in nature; thus upon each other, from our own point of liberty. And accordingly society is, in all its vast complications, an appointment—we can not escape it. We can only say what kind of experience it shall be as regards the fruits of character in us. Meantime God is reigning over it, socially related Himself to each member, governing and training that member through his own liberty. Life, thus ordered, is a magnificent scheme to bring out the value of law and teach the necessity of right as the only conserving principle of order and happiness; teaching the more powerfully that it teaches, if so it must, by disorder and sorrow. And nature, it will be observed, is the universal medium by or through which the training is accomplished. The powers act on each other, by acting on the lines of cause and effect in nature; starting thus new trains of events and consequences, by which they affect each other, in ways of injury or blessing. They speak and set the air in motion, as it otherwise would not move; and so the obedient air, played on by their sovereignty, becomes the vehicle of words that communicate innumerable stings, insults, flatteries, seductions, threats; or tones of comfort, love and blessing. So of all the other elements, solid, fluid, or aerial—they are medial as between the powers. The whole play of commerce in society is through nature, and is in fact a playing on the causes and objects of nature by supernatural agents. All doings and misdoings are, in this view, a kind of discourse in the terms of nature, by which these supernatural agents, viz., men, answer to each other, or to God, in society. Their blasphemies and prayers and songs and threats, their looks and gestures, their dress and manners, their injuries and alms, their blows and barricades and bullets and bombs, these and such like are society, the grand conversation by which our social discipline is carried on. And it is all a supernatural transaction. As a conversation in words is not reducible to mere natural causation, no more is that conversation in bullets and bombs that we call a battle. Nature could as well talk, as compound her forces in cartridges and fire them with a leveled aim. Her activity in all these exchanges, or medial transactions, that are carried on so briskly, is only the activity of the powers through her, and is, in fact, supernatural. . . .

# THE ATONEMENT

## From *God in Christ*,

## "A Discourse on the Atonement" (1849)*

I John, i. 2.—"For the Life was manifested, and we have seen it,
and bear witness, and shew unto you that eternal life which was
with the Father, and was manifested unto us."

This particular passage of scripture has seemed to me to offer one of
the most comprehensive and most deliberate announcements of the doctrine of Christ, that is anywhere given in the sacred writings, with the
advantage that it is yet so far unoccupied as not to have become a tech-
nic, under the wear of any theory. In the verse previous, the writer
opens by setting forth the fact, as I suppose, of a divine incarnation in
the person of Jesus. By the Word, or Word of Life, that peculiar power
in the Divine nature by which God is able to represent Himself outwardly in the forms of things, first in the worlds and now in the human
person, which is the liveliest type of feeling possible, and closest to
God—by this Word of Life, God has now expressed Himself. He has set
forth His Divine feeling even to sense and as a fellow-feeling—He has
entered into human history, as one of its biographic elements. We have
seen, looked upon, handled what may thus be known of Him. Then, he
adds—throwing in a parenthesis which is to be a solution of the whole
evangelic history—"for the Life was manifested, and we have seen it,
and bear witness, and shew unto you that Eternal Life, which was with
the Father, and was manifested unto us."

Observe three points in this very peculiar language. First, there is a
manifestation of something, the mission of the Word is looked upon
inclusively as a manifestation, that is, a coming into visibility of something before invisible. Secondly, it is the Life that was manifested—not
life generally speaking, but *the* Life. And, thirdly, as if to distinguish it
in a yet more definite manner, it is called *that* Life, that Eternal Life,
that Eternal Life that was *with* the Father, and was manifested unto us.

Taking, now, these three terms, in connection with the assumption,
elsewhere made, that our human race, under sin, are alienated from the

* [Ed.] *God in Christ* (Hartford: Brown and Parsons, 1849), pp. 185–275. Included here:
pp. 187–95, 202–16, 246–58, 266–68.

life of God; also, with the declaration of Christ, that, as the Father hath life in Himself, so he hath given to the Son, as the world's Redeemer, to have life in himself; and, again, with that deep utterance of joy sent forth by an emancipated soul;—"for the law of the spirit of life in Christ Jesus, hath made me free from the law of sin and death"*—taking the text, I say, in connection with these others, as commentaries, we have a good synoptic view, it seems to me, of the doctrine of the Messiah.

It is not that Christ is a man, a human teacher, who is sent to reform us by his words and his beautiful human example, but it is to this effect:—All souls have their proper life only in the common vivifying life of God. Sin, being a withdrawal into self and self-hood, separates them from the life, and, as far as their own freedom is concerned, denies all influx of the Divine into their character and their religious nature. Passing thus into a state of negation, as regards the Divine all-sustaining life, they become imprisoned in darkness, unbelief, idolatry, and a general captivity to sense. And now the Life is manifested in sense; in Christ is life, and the life is the light of men. Christ enters into human feeling, by his incarnate charities and sufferings, to re-engage the world's love and reunite the world, as free, to the Eternal Life. To sum up all in one condensed and luminous utterance, every word of which is power, *God was in Christ, reconciling the world unto Himself.*† The apostle says nothing here, it will be observed, of reconciling God to men, he only speaks of reconciling men to God. Had he said "the Life of God was manifested in Jesus Christ, to quicken the world in love and truth, and reunite it to Himself," he would have said the same thing under a different form.

I am well aware that, in offering such a statement, as the true doctrine of Christ and his work, I affirm nothing that is distinctively orthodox, and shall even seem to rule out that view of Christ as a *sacrifice*, an *expiation for sin*, a *vicarious offering*, which, to the view of most orthodox Christians, contains the real import of his work as a Saviour. It will be found, however, that I am proceeding exactly in the line of the scriptures, and I trust also it will appear, before I have done, that the scriptures advance two distinct views of Christ and his work, which are yet radically one and the same.

I. A subjective, speculative—one that contemplates the work of Christ in its ends, and views it as a power related to its ends.

II. An objective, ritualistic—one that sets him forth to faith, instead of philosophy, and one, without which, as an Altar Form for the soul, he would not be the power intended, or work the ends appointed.

Thus, when it is inquired, as in the first form specified, for what end

---

* [Ed.] Romans 8:2.
† [Ed.] II Corinthians 5:19.

did Christ come into the world, we have a class of terms in the scripture which can scarcely get any proper meaning, if what is said under the second form is considered to be the whole doctrine of Christ. The converse also is equally true. The real problem is to find a place and a meaning for *all* that is said concerning him—to effect a union of the two sides. . . .

But before I engage more immediately in the effort thus undertaken, it may be useful to glance, a moment, at some of the opinions that have been held or advanced, at different times, concerning the nature and import of the atonement. . . . There is a general concurrence in the words *vicarious, expiation, offering, substitute,* and the like, but no agreement as to the manner in which they are to get their meaning. Sometimes, the analogy of criminal law is taken; and then our sins are spoken of as being transferred to Christ, or he as having accepted them to bear their penalty. Sometimes the civil or commercial law furnishes the analogy; and then our sins, being taken as a debt, Christ offers himself as a ransom for us. Or, the analogy of the ceremonial law is accepted; and then Christ is set forth as a propitiatory, or expiatory offering, to obtain remission of sins for us. Regarding Christ as suffering for us, in one or another of these scripture forms or figures, taken as the literal dogmatic truth, we have as many distinct theories. Then, again, different as these figures are from each other, they will yet be used interchangeably, all in the sense of one or another of them. And then, again, to double the confusion yet once more, we have two sets of representations produced under each, accordingly as Christ is conceived to offer himself to Jehovah's justice, or as Jehovah is conceived Himself to prepare the offering, out of His own mercy.

On the whole, I know of no definite and fixed point, on which the orthodox view, so called, may be said to hang, unless it be this, viz., that Christ suffers evil as evil, or in direct and simple substitution for evil that was to be suffered by us; so that God accepts one evil in place of the other, and being satisfied in this manner, is able to justify or pardon.

As to the measure of this evil, there are different opinions. Calvin maintained the truly horrible doctrine that Christ descended into hell, when crucified, and suffered the pains of the damned for three days. A very great number of the Christian teachers, even at this day, maintain that Christ suffered exactly as much pain as all the redeemed would have suffered under the penalties of eternal justice. But this penal view of Christ's death has been gradually giving way, till now, under its most modern, most mitigated and least objectionable form, he is only said to have suffered under a law of *expression.*

Thus, God would have expressed a certain abhorrence of sin, by the punishment of the world. Christ now suffers only as much pain as will express the same amount of abhorrence. And considering the dignity of the sufferer, and his relations to the Father, there was no need of suffering the same, or even any proximate amount of pain, to make an expression of abhorrence to sin, that is, of justice, equal to that produced by the literal punishment of the race. Still, it will be seen to be a part of this more mitigated view, that Christ suffers evil as evil, which evil suffered is accepted as a compensative expression of God's indignation against sin. . . .

[(Ed.) I omit Bushnell's detailed criticisms of both the classical substitutionary theory of atonement (as developed by Anselm and Calvin) and the more modern "expressive" theory (attributed to Hugo Grotius). (For a discussion of the uneasy co-existence of these theories in New England theology, see Dorus Paul Rudisill, *The Doctrine of the Atonement in Jonathan Edwards and His Successors* [New York: Poseidon Books, 1971].) In his discussion, Bushnell deftly identified internal inconsistencies in the theories. However, his major objection to both concerned the "moral repugnance" he believed any right-minded person would feel at the notion that God would have made Christ suffer punishment for sins he did not commit. In this, Bushnell echoed the tone and substance of Unitarian critiques of Calvinism: e.g., William Ellery Channing, "The Moral Argument Against Calvinism," *The Works of William Ellery Channing, D.D.* (Boston: American Unitarian Association, 1897), pp. 459–68.]

Having stated frankly these objections to the common orthodox views of atonement, whether resting the value of Christ's death in what it *is*, or in what it *expresses*, it may be expected that I should renounce all sympathy and connection with them. This I have never been able to do. For if they are unsatisfactory, if the older and more venerable doctrine is repugnant, when speculatively regarded, to the most sacred instincts or sentiments of our moral nature, and dissolves itself at the first approach of rational inquiry, is it nothing remarkable, is it not even more remarkable, that it should have supported the spirit of so many believers and martyrs, in so many trials and deaths, continued through so many centuries? Refuted again and again, cast away, trampled upon by irreverent mockeries, it has never yet been able to die—wherefore, unless there be some power of divine life in it? So I have always believed, and I hope to show you, before I have done, where it is, or under what form it is hid; for I shall carry you into a region, separate from all speculation, or theologizing, and there, what I now dismiss, I shall virtually reclaim and restore, in a shape that provokes none of these objections. All that is real and essential to the power of this orthodox doctrine of atonement, however held, I hope to set forth still, as the DIVINE FORM of Christianity, assigning it a place where it may still reveal its efficacy, standing even as an Altar of penitence and peace, a Pillar of confidence to believing souls.

We come now to the double view of the atonement, or work of Christ, which it was proposed to establish. And,

I. The subjective, that which represents Christ as a manifestation of the Life, thus a power whose end it is to quicken, or regenerate the human character.

Here, as it has been already intimated, the value of Christ's mission is measured by what is expressed. And if so, then it follows, of course, that no dogmatic statement can adequately represent his work; for the matter of it does not lie in formulas of reason, and cannot be comprehended in them. It is more a poem than a treatise. It classes as a work of Art more than as a work of Science. It addresses the understanding, in great part, through the feeling or sensibility. In these it has its receptivities, by these it is perceived, or perceivable. Moving, in and through these, as a revelation of sympathy, love, life, it proposes to connect us with the Life of God. And when through these, believingly opened as inlets, it is received, then is the union it seeks consummated. Were it not for the air it might give to my representations, in the view of many, I should like, in common with Paul, (Phil. i. 9, 10.) to use the word *esthetic*, and represent Christianity as a power moving upon man, through this department of his nature, both to regenerate his degraded perception of excellence, and also to communicate, in that way, the fullness and beauty of God.

Hence, it would not be as wild a breach of philosophy itself, to undertake a dogmatic statement of the contents of a tragedy, as to attempt giving in the same manner the equivalents of the life and death of Jesus Christ. The only real equivalent we can give is the representation of the life itself. It is not absurd, however, to say something about the subject, if only we do not assume the adequacy of what we say—we could offer some theoretical views of a tragedy, but our theoretic matter would not be the tragedy. No more can we set forth, as a real and proper equivalent, any theoretic matter of ours concerning the life and death of Jesus Christ, which is the highest and most moving tragedy ever acted in this mortal sphere; a tragedy distinguished in the fact that God is the Chief Character, and the divine feeling, moved in tragic earnest—Goodness Infinite manifested through Sorrow—the passion represented.

Beginning, then, with the lowest view our subject permits, it is obvious that the life of Christ, considered only as a perfect being or character, is an embodiment in human history, of a spirit and of ideas, which are sufficient of themselves to change the destinies of the race, and even their capabilities of good. Is it too much for me to assume that Christ was such a character? Is it intimated that a very close, microscopic inspection has revealed, as some imagine, two or three flaws in his life? Be it so; I want no other evidence that he was a perfect and sinless being. Sin is never revealed microscopically, but, wherever it is, it sets its mark, as we set our flag on a new-discovered island. Show me, therefore, a character that is flawed only microscopically, and I will charge the flaws to the microscope or even to the solar beam, rather than to it. Christ, then, I assume, was a sinlessly perfect being. And how great an event, to have had one such perfect life or biography lived and witnessed in the world, and so deposited in the bosom of our human history. Here we have among us, call him either human only, or divine, what the most splendid gifts of human genius had labored in vain to sketch—a perfect life. What feelings, principles, beauties, ideas or regulative ideals, are thus imported into the world's bosom! Only to have seen one perfect life, to have heard the words and received the pure conceptions of one sinless spirit, to have felt the working of his charities, and witnessed the offering of his sinless obedience, would have been to receive the seeds of a moral revolution that must ultimately affect the whole race. This was true even of a Socrates. Our world is not the same world that it was before he lived in it. Much less the same, since the sinless Jesus lived and suffered in it. Such a character has, of necessity, an organific power. It enters into human thought and knowledge as a vital force; and since it is perfect, a vital force that cannot die, or cease to work. It must, of necessity, organize a kingdom of life, and reign. The ideas it has revealed, and the spirit it has breathed into the air, are quick and powerful, and must live till the world itself is no more. The same sun may shine above, the same laws of nature may reign about us, but the grand society of man embodies new elemental forces, and the capacity, at some time or other, of another and a gloriously renovated state. The entering of one such perfect life into the world's history changes, in fact, the consciousness of the race. . . .

But if we are to understand the full import of Christ's mission, we must go farther. He is not merely a perfect life embodied in history. He is not merely the Eternal Life manifested in a good and upright history. We must regard him as the Life manifested in an evil history, or that of an alienated and averted race. He finds us under sin, captives imprisoned by evil, and he comes to be our liberator. Accordingly, we are now to see in what manner he addresses himself to the moral wants and disabilities of a state of sin.

And here, glancing first of all at human society, we discover the appalling fact that sin, once existing, becomes, and even must become, a corporate authority—a law or Ruling Power, in the world, opposite to God. Entering into the fashions, opinions, manners, ends, passions of the race, it molds their institutions, legislates over their conduct, and even constructs a morality by standards of its own. And thus, acting through the mass, it becomes a law to the individual, crowning Lust and Mammon as gods, harnessing nations to the chariot of war, building thrones of oppression, kindling fires of persecution, poisoning the fountains of literature, adorning falsehood with the splendors of genius, sanctifying wrong under the plausible names of honor and fashion. Thus, or by all these methods, sin becomes a kind of malign possession in the race, a prince of the power of the air, reigning unto death. To break the organic force of social evil, thus dominant over the race, Christ enters the world, bringing into human history and incorporating in it as such, that which is Divine. The Life manifested in him becomes a historic power and presence in the world's bosom, organizing there a new society or kingdom, called the kingdom of heaven, or sometimes the church. For the church is not a body of men holding certain dogmas, or maintaining, as men, certain theologic wars for God; but it is the Society of the Life, the Embodied Word. Thus it is expressly declared to be the body of Christ, the fullness of him that filleth all in all. Hence our blessed Lord, just before his passion, considering that now the organic force of evil was to be broken, said, now is the judgment of this world, now is the prince of this world cast out. The princedom of evil is dissolved—the eternal Life, manifested in the world, organizes a new society of life, breaks the spell forever of social evil, and begins a reign of truth and love that shall finally renew the world. . . .

The manifestation of the Life also revives in man, as a sinner, the consciousness of himself. It is one of the paradoxes realized by sin, that, while it makes a man every thing to himself, it makes him also nothing. It smothers the spark of conscious immortality. This world is practically all to him. The grave is dark, and he has no faith to throw a light across on spiritual realities beyond it. But when he that was in the form of God comes into the human state, when we see one here who visibly is not of us, when he opens here a heart of love, and floods the world with rivers of divine feeling, when we trace him from the manger over which the hymns of heaven's joy are ringing, to the cross where his purpose to save embraces even death for man; and then, when we see that death cannot hold him, that he bursts into life again as a victor over death—following such a history transacted, in our view, we begin also to conceive the tremendous import of our own, the equally tremendous import also of our sin. If God, to renew the soul moves a plan like this, what is it to be a soul, what to desecrate and destroy a soul? The conscious grandeur of his eternity returns upon the transgressor and he trembles in awe of himself—himself the power of an endless life.

Suppose, now, to advance another stage, that a man under sin becomes reflective, conscious of himself and of evil, sighing with discontent and bitterness, because of his own spiritual disorders. Conceive him thus as undertaking a restoration of his own nature to goodness, and the pure ideal of his conscience. What can he do without some objective power to engage his affections, and be a higher nature, present, by which to elevate and assimilate his own? Sin has removed him from God; withdrawing into himself, his soul has become objectless, and good affections cannot live, or be made to live, where there is no living object left to warm and support them. He can rise, therefore, by no help from his affections, or through them. Accordingly, if he attempts to restore himself to that ideal beauty and purity he has lost, he is obliged to do it wholly by his will; possibly against the depressing bondage of his affections, now sunk in torpor and deadness, or soured by a protracted, malign activity. Having all this to do by his will, he finds, alas! that if to will is present, how to perform is not. He seems, to himself, like a man who is endeavoring to lift himself by pulling at his feet. Hence, or to remove this disability, God needs to be manifested as Love. The Divine Object rejected by sin and practically annihilated as a spiritual conception, needs to be imported into sense. Then when God appears in His beauty, loving and lovely, the good, the glory, the sunlight of soul, the affections, previously dead, wake into life and joyful play, and what before was only a self-lifting and slavish effort becomes an exulting spirit of liberty. The body of sin and death that lay upon the soul is heaved off, and the law of the spirit of life in Christ Jesus—the Eternal Life manifested in him, and received by faith into a vital union—quickens it in good, and makes it free.

But there is yet another difficulty, over and above the deadness and the moral estrangement of the affections; I speak of the fearful and self-accusing spirit of sin. Reason as we may about human depravity, apologize for men, or justify them as we may, they certainly do not justify themselves. Even in the deepest mental darkness concerning God, stifled, we may almost say, as regards their proper humanity, under the sottish and debasing effects of idolatry, still we see the conscience struggling with guilty fears, unable to find the rest. An indescribable dread of evil still overhangs the human spirit. The being is haunted by shadows of wrath and tries all painful methods of self pacification. Vigils, pilgrimages, sacrifices, tortures, nothing is too painful or wearisome that promises to ease the guilt of the mind. Without any speculations about justification, mankind refuse to justify themselves. A kind of despair fills the heart of the race. They have no courage. Whether they know God or not, they know themselves, and they sentence themselves to death. If they have only some obscure notions of a divine Being, then they dread the full discovery of Him. If He lurks in their gods, they fear lest their gods should visit them in vengence, or plague them by some kind of mischief. The sky is full of wrathful powers, and the deep ground also is full. Their guilty soul peoples the world with vengeful images of its own creation.

And here, now, if we desire to find it, is the true idea of Christian justification. We discover what it is by the want of it. Justification is that which will give confidence, again, to guilty minds; that which will assure the base and humiliated soul of the world, chase away the demons of wrath and despair it has evoked, and help it to return to God in courage, whispering still to itself—soul be of good cheer, thy sins are forgiven thee.

And this result is beautifully prepared by the advent of Christ, as well as by the crowning act of his death. God thus enters humanity as the Word made flesh, and unites himself to it, declaring by that sign, that he is ready to unite it unto himself. We perceive also and hear that he has come, not to condemn the world, but to save it. No storm wraps him about when he comes. The hymn that proclaims him, publishes—"peace on earth." He appears in a form to indicate the gentlest errand and the closest approach to our human lot; one, too, that never appalls the guiltiest—the form of a child. In his ministry he sometimes utters piercing words, still he is a friend, even a brother to the guilty. He calls the heavy-laden to come unto him, and promises rest. In short, he lives confidence into the world. Apart from all theologic theories, we know, we see with our eyes, that God will justify us and give us still his peace. And then, when we truly come unto him, believing that Christ the Word is He, when, forsaking all things for him, we embrace him as our life, then are we practically justified. It is impossible for us to fear. No guilt of the past can disturb us, a peace that passeth understanding fills our nature. Being justified by faith, we have peace with God through our Lord Jesus Christ.

Or, if we advert, in this connection, to the sufferings and death of Christ, we shall see how these, without the imputation of any penal quality or crown of God upon his person, have a special efficacy in fortifying our assurance or hope of justification with God. Dismiss all speculation about the mode, possibility, interior reality of this suffering; understand that God, having proposed, in this manner, to express His love, all logical, theological, ontological, physiological questions are, by the supposition, out of place. Come, then, to the spectacle of Christ's suffering life and death, as to a mystery wholly transcendent, save in what it expresses of Divine feeling. Call what of this feeling you receive the reality—all else the *machina Dei* for the expression of this. With deepest reverence of soul, approach that most mysterious sacrament of love, the agony of Jesus; note the patience of his trial, the meekness of his submission to injustice, and the malignant passions of his enemies; behold the creation itself darkening and shuddering with a horror of sensibility at the scene transpiring in his death; hear the cry of the crucified—"Father, forgive them, for they know not what they do;" then regard the life that was manifested, dropping into cessation, and thereby signifying the deposit of itself in the bosom of that malign world, to whose enmity it is yielded—who, what man of our race beholding this strange history of the Word, will not feel a new courage enter into his soul? Visibly, God is not the implacable avenger his guilty fears had painted. But he is a friend, he is low. And so great is this change, apart from all theology, that I seem even to see another character produced by it, in the Christian nations. They dare to hope. God is closer to them and in a way to inspire courage. They are not withered, humiliated even to baseness, under those guilty and abject fears that take away at last the spirit of other nations. It is not that they have all a theory of justification by faith, but that their current conceptions of God are such as the history of Jesus, the suffering redeemer, has imparted. They have a feeling of something like justification, even if they never heard of it—a feeling, which, if it were to vent itself in language, would say—Therefore we are freely justified by grace. It is not that the suffering appeases God, but that it expresses God—displays, in open history, the unconquerable love of God's Heart. . . .

This brings me to the—

II. Department of my subject, that in which I proposed to unfold an objective ritual view, answering to the more speculative and subjective now presented, and necessary, as such, to the full effect and power of Christ's mission.

Few persons are aware how intently our mental instinct labors to throw all its subjects of thought and feeling into objectivity. For we think, in the liveliest manner, only when we get our thoughts out of us, if I may so speak, and survey them as before us. Thus we say of a scene, that it was *pitiful*, or *joyful*, or *delightful*, not because the scene itself was really full of pity, joy, or delight, but because we were so ourselves. Still we do not say it, but we give objectivity to our feeling, passing over our pity, joy, delight, into the scene, and having it for our pleasure to see the feeling there. So we say that a thing is *grateful* to us, when we mean that we are grateful for it; and, in the same manner, we call a man a *suspicious* character, when we only mean that we are suspicious, or may well be suspicious of him. We even throw our own acts into objectivity. Thus the word *attribute* properly denotes an act of *attributing* or *imputing* in us, but we use it as having no subjective reference whatever. We even make our own thinking processes objective, in the same manner, saying, *it occurs to us, it appears to us*, when, in fact, we are only describing what transpires within us. Human language, indeed, is full of illustrations to the same effect, showing how it is the constant effort of our nature to work itself, report its thoughts and play its sentiments, under forms of representation that are objective.

Accordingly, it will be found that all the religions the world has ever seen, have taken, as it were by instinct, an objective form. No race of men, so far as I know, have ever undertaken to work their sentiments towards God or the gods artificially; that is, by a reflective operation, or by addressing their own nature, under the philosophic laws of moral effect. The religion has been wholly an outward transaction, not in form a transaction of the soul. It has worked the soul only in a manner somewhat unconscious, or by a kind of silent implication. Ask the worshipper what is the religion, and he will say, it is the sacrifice offered thus or thus, the procession, the vow, the priestly ceremony—some objective pageant or transaction. He probably conceives no such thing as a subjective effect, distinct from what he sees with his eyes; still there is such an effect, and it is only in virtue of this, received in a latent or unconscious manner, that the transaction seen by the eyes has any significance to him.

Such, as we may see at a glance, was the religion of the Jewish people. It stood, not in subjective exercises carefully stated and logically distinguished, but in a carefully exact ritual of outward exercise. Their religion, if closely studied, will be found to consist of artistic matter wholly above their invention—a scheme of ritualities so adjusted as to work sentiments, states, and moral effects in the worshippers, which, as yet, they were unable to conceive or speak of themselves. It had a mystic power wholly transcendent, as regards their own understanding, and one that involved an insight so profound, of the relation of form to sentiment, that God only could have prepared it. Manifestly it was impossible for a people so little exercised in reflection, to make any thing of a religion which consisted in reflecting on themselves, conceiving, then addressing their wants, by intellectual motives. Working thus upon themselves, in the manner of 'Edwards on the Affections,'* what could the men whom Moses led out of Egypt have done? But they had their 'Edwards on the Affections' in altars, unblemished bullocks and lambs, bloody sprinklings, smokes rolling up to heaven, and solemn feasts; and counting these to be their religion, beyond which they could hardly manage a religious thought of any kind, there was yet an artistic power in their rites, such that in being simply transacted, they carried impressions, so efficacious in the production of a religious spirit, that many, without the least conception of religion as a subjective experience, were undoubtedly brought into a state of real penitence and vital union with

---

* [Ed.] Jonathan Edwards' *Treatise on the Religious Affections* was sometimes used in Bushnell's day as a manual of religious self-examination. For Bushnell's critique of introspective methods for fostering piety or judging the authenticity of conversion, see "Self-Examination Examined," *Sermons on Living Subjects* (New York: Scribner, Armstrong & Co., 1872), pp. 224–42.

God. Having no philosophy of the moral government of God; without any conception whatever of law, in the higher sense, or of sin, justification, faith, and spiritual life; the ritual came into their feeling when transacted, with a wisdom they had not in their understanding, and their soul received impressions under the artistic objectivities of the altar, which, by reason or intellectual contemplation, they were wholly unable to comprehend. In the progress of their history, they visibly become more reflective, speaking oftener of that which lies in the state of the heart, and the internal aim and principle of the life. Still they had never gone so far, previous to the coming of Christ, as to conceive a purely subjective religion.

Nor is that any proper and true conception of Christianity. Some persons appear to suppose that Christianity is distinguished by the fact that it has finally cleared us of all ritualities or objectivities, introducing a purely subjective and philosophic or ideal piety. This they fancy is the real distinction between Judaism and Christianity. They do not conceive that Christianity rather fulfills Judaism than displaces it—that, while it dismisses the *outward* rites and objectivities of the old religion, it does, in fact, erect them into so many *inward* objectivities, and consecrate them as the Divine Form of the Christian grace for all future time. Thus, instead of a religion before the eyes, we now have one set up in language before the mind's eye, one that is almost as intensely objective as the other, only that it is mentally so, or as addressed to thought. The sacrifices and other Jewish machineries are gone, yet they are all here—indeed they never found their true significance, till Christ came and took them up into their higher use, as vehicles of his divine truth. The scheme of God is one, not many. The positive institutions, rites, historic processes of the ante-Christian ages are all so many preparations made by the transcendent wisdom of God, with a secret design to bring forth, when it is wanted, a divine form for the Christian truth—which, if we do not perceive, the historic grandeur of Christianity is well nigh lost.

Then, also, and for the same reason, is the sublime art of Christianity concealed from us. We do not conceive it as art, but only as a didactic power, a doctrine, a divine philosophy. Whereas a great part of its dignity and efficacy consists in the artistic power of its form as an objective religion—a religion *for* the soul and *before* it, so intensely efficient to operate a religion in it. And this, precisely, is the defect of the subjective view I have presented. It offers no altar Form for the soul's worship, but only something to be received by consideration—such a kind of remedy for sin that, if we had it on hand always to act reflectively, and administer to our own moral disease, it would be well. But that is not the remedy that meets our case. Just as the sick man wants, not an apothecary, but a physician; not a store of drugs out of which he may choose and apply for himself, but to commit himself, in trust, to one who shall administer for him, and watch the working of his cure: so the soul that is under sin wants to deposit her being in an objective mercy, to let go self-amendment, to believe, and in her faith to live. . . .

There is no doubt that the Hebrew people, whose religion was so intensely objective, held it in a manner of literality that involved real misconception. They saw nothing in it but the altars, priests, confessions, sprinklings and smoking fires, and these they called their atonement, or the covering of their sin; as if there were some outward value in the things themselves—taken outwardly these were the religion. But, meantime, there was a power in these, by which subjective effects were continually transpiring within them, and the outward value of the rite, which was a fiction, had yet an inward value correspondent thereto, which made the fiction truthful. There was a re-acting power, a power to produce reflex impressions in the rites, by which the law was sanctified; by which they testified and were made to feel repentance for sin; by which they were exercised in faith to receive the remission of sins. They had their religion, as they thought, in their altar, which conciliated God to them; and what they had, as they thought, before their eyes, was a religious experience in their hearts. This, at least, was the plan, though it was possible for them to fail of the true result, as it is for us, under a more reflective and self-regulative form of piety. They were to deposit their soul in the outward rite, and there to let it rest; and then the outward rite was relied upon to be a power in the heart. The plan was, to frame a religion that would produce its results artistically; that is, immediately, without reflection, by the mere liturgic force of forms. Endowed with an artistic power, these forms were to work their impression, in the immediate, absolute way that distinguishes art, and without the interposition of thought, debate, choice, and self-application. Thus the Jew had, in effect, a whole religion present to thought, when he simply looked upon the *blood* of his victim; and yet in a manner so transcendent, in one view so mystical, that when we endeavor to analyze the import of the word *blood*, and tell by what element or elements it becomes thus expressive, we find it difficult, by any circumlocutions that avoid the altar and the sacrificial images, to say any thing that shall exactly represent our impressions. This same artistic force or immediateness of impression, is obviously as much more to be desired in Christianity, as the subjective truths and powers it contains have a vaster moment.

Passing, now, into the domain of Christianity, let us try an experiment on the subjective doctrine already exhibited, and see how far it may be represented in objective equivalents drawn from the ancient ritual. Christ, we have seen, is a power for the moral renovation of the world, and as such is measured by what he expresses. Thus we have seen that by his obedience, by the expense and painstaking of his suffering life, by the yielding up of his own sacred person to die, he has produced

in us a sense of the eternal sanctity of God's law that was needful to
prevent a growth of license or of indifference and insensibility to religious obligation, such as must be incurred, if the exactness and rigor of a
law-system were wholly dissipated, by offers of pardon grounded in
mere leniency. The moral propriety, then, or possibility, nay, in one
view, the ground of justification, is subjectively prepared in us; viz., in a
state or impression, a sense of the sacredness of law, produced in us, by
Christ's life and death. But we cannot think of it in this artificial way;
most persons could make nothing of it. We must transfer this subjective
state or impression, this ground of justification, and produce it outwardly, if possible, in some objective form; as if it had some effect on
the law or on God. The Jew had done the same before us, and we follow
him; representing Christ as our sacrifice, sin-offering, atonement, or
sprinkling of blood. Now in all these terms, we represent a work as done
outwardly for us, which is really done in us, and through impressions
prepared in us, but the more adequately and truly still, for the reason
that we have it in mystic forms before us. These forms are the objective
equivalents of our subjective impressions. Indeed, our impressions have
their life and power in and under these forms. Neither let it be imagined
that we only happen to seize upon these images of sacrifice, atonement,
and blood, because they are at hand. They are prepared, as God's form
of art, for the representation of Christ and his work; and if we refuse to
let him pass into this form, we have no mold of thought that can fitly
represent him. And when he is thus represented, we are to understand
that he is our sacrifice and atonement, that by his blood we have remission, not in any speculative sense, but as in art. We might as well think
to come at the statue of Aristides speculatively, interpreting its power by
geometric demonstrations, instead of giving our heart to the expression
of integrity in the form, as to be scheming and dogmatizing over these
words *atonement, sin-offering, sacrifice,* and *blood,* which are the divine
form of Christianity. . . .

You perceive, in this manner, and as a result of our experiment, that
as soon as we undertake to throw the elements of our subjective doctrine
into an objective representation, it passes immediately into the view
commonly designated by the phrase *vicarious atonement,* only it rather
becomes a vicarious religion. And thus, after all, it proves itself to be
identical, at the root, with the common Protestant doctrine—identical, I
mean, not in any rigid and exact sense, but in such a sense that one is
more didactic and reflective, the other a more artistic representation of
the same subject matter. There is no conflict, until we begin to assert the
former as the only truth of the gospel, or to work up the latter by itself,
into a speculative system of dogma or of moral government. If we say
that Christ is here, reconciling men to God, it is, for just that reason,
necessary to have a way of representing that God is conciliated towards

us. If we say that Christ is a power, to quicken us into newness of life, and bring us out of the bondage we are under to evil, for just that reason do we need to speak of the remission of sins obtained by his blood; for the two seem to be only different forms of one and the same truth, and are often run together in the scriptures—as when the blood of Christ, "who offered himself without spot to God," is said "to purge the conscience from dead works, to serve the living God." The two views are not logically or theologically equivalent, but they are not the less really so on that account. An objective religion that shall stand before me, and be operated or operative for me, excluding all subjective reference of thought, must take such forms most obviously, as are no logical equivalents of the same, considered as addressing and describing our internal states; for, by the supposition, an objective artistic power is substituted for those methods of address which appeal to consideration, reflection, and self-regulation. . . .

[W]e may be confident that, as our spirit becomes more sanctified and assimilated to God, we shall become more spontaneous in good, and have less need to be acting reflectively. But, in order ever to become thus spontaneous, we need, when we are least so, to be exercised objectively, thus to forget and go clear of ourselves; otherwise our piety, so called, settles into a mere dressing of the soul before her mirror. It is millinery substituted for grace. If the soul, then, is ever to get her health and freedom in goodness, she must have the gospel, not as a doctrine only, but as a rite before her, a righteousness, a ransom, a sacrifice, a lamb slain, a blood offered for her cleansing before Jehovah's altar. Then, reclining her broken heart on this, calling it her religion—hers by faith—she receives a grace broader than consciousness, loses herself in a love that is not imparted in the molds of mere self-culture, and, without making folly of Christ by her own vain self-applications, he is made *unto her*, wisdom, righteousness, sanctification, and redemption.

I might speak, also, in this connection, of the sad figure that would be made by the rude masses of the world, in applying a gospel of philosophic causes to their own nature; for they hardly know, as yet, that they have a nature. How manifest is it that they want an altar, set up before them, and if they cannot quite see the blood of Christ sprinkled on it, they must have it as a FORM in their souls; he must be a stock of righteousness before them; he must bear their sins for them, and be, in fact, their religion. Then, taking him, by faith, to be all this before and for them, the Divine Art hid in it transforms their inner life, in the immediate, absolute manner of art; and seeing now their new peace, not in themselves where it is, but in God, they rejoice that God is reconciled, and His anger smoothed away.

However, there is no such difference of class, among men, that the most cultivated and wisest disciple will not often need, and as often rejoice, to get away from all self-handling and self-cherishing cares. To be rid of a reflective and artificial activity, to fall into utter simplicity, and let the soul repose herself in a love and confidence wholly artless, is not only to be desired, but it is necessary, as I have said, even to the quality of true goodness itself. To be ever lifting ourselves by our will, to be hanging round our own works, canvassing our defects, studying the pathology of our own evils, were enough, of itself, to drive one mad. The mind becomes wearied and lost in its own mazes, discouraged and crushed by its frequent defeats, and virtue itself, being only a conscious tug of exertion, takes a look as unbeautiful as the life is unhappy. Therefore we need, all alike, some objective religion; to come and hang ourselves upon the altar of sacrifice sprinkled by the blood of Jesus, to enter into the holiest set open by his death, to quiet our soul in his peace, clothe it in his righteousness, and trust him as the Lamb of God that taketh away our sin. In these simple, unselfish, unreflective exercises, we shall make our closest approach to God.

# From *The Vicarious Sacrifice* (1866)*

It is matter of sorrowful indication, that the thing most wanting to be cleared in Christianity is still, as it ever has been, the principal thing; viz., the meaning and method of reconciliation itself, or of what is commonly called the vicarious sacrifice. This fact would even be itself a considerable evidence against the Gospel, were it not that the subject-matter—so vast in the reach of its complications, and so nearly transcendent in the height of its reasons—yields up easily to faith its practical significance, when refusing to be theoretically mastered, as yet, by the understanding.

There has been a litigation of the sacrifice going on for these eighteen hundred years, and especially for the last eight hundred; yet still it remains an open question with many, whether any such thing as vicarious sacrifice pertains to the work of salvation Christ has accomplished. On one side the fact is abjured as irrational and revolting. On the other it is affirmed as a principal fact of the Christian salvation; though I feel obliged to confess that it is too commonly maintained under definitions and forms of argument that make it revolting.† And which of the two is the greater wrong and most to be deplored, that by which the fact itself is rejected, or that by which it is made fit to be rejected, I will not stay to discuss. Enough that Christianity, in either way, suffers incalculable loss; or must, if there be any such principal matter in it, as I most certainly believe that there is.

Assuming now, for the subject of this treatise, the main question stated, our first point must be to settle a just and true conception of vicarious sacrifice, or of what is the real undertaking of Christ in the matter of such sacrifice. For in all such matter, the main issue is commonly decided by adjusting other and better conceptions of the question itself, and not by forcing old ones through into victory, by the artillery practice of better contrived arguments.

This word *vicarious*, that has made so conspicuous a figure in the

---

* [Ed.] *The Vicarious Sacrifice Grounded in Principles of Universal Obligation* (New York: Charles Scribner & Co., 1866). This book later became volume I of a two volume set, also called *The Vicarious Sacrifice* (1877), which included *Forgiveness and Law* as its second volume. Included here: pp. 3–13.

† The two "sides" Bushnell has in mind are the Unitarians and the Calvinists, respectively.

debates of theology, it must be admitted is no word of the Scripture. The same is true, however, of *free agency, character, theology,* and of many other terms which the conveniences of use have made common. If a word appears to be wanted in Christian discussions or teachings, the fact that it is not found in the Scripture is no objection to it; we have only to be sure that we understand what we mean by it. In the case, too, of this particular word *vicarious,* a special care is needed, lest we enter something into the meaning, from ourselves, which is not included in the large variety of Scripture terms and expressions the word is set to represent.

Thus we have—"made a curse for us"—"bare our sins"—"hath laid on him the iniquity of us all"—"made to be sin for us"—"offered to bear the sins of many"—"borne our griefs and carried our sorrows"—"wounded for our transgressions, bruised for our iniquities"—"tasted death for every man." The whole Gospel is a texture, thus, of vicarious conceptions in which Christ is represented, in one way or another, as coming into our place, substituted in our stead, bearing our burdens, answering for us, and standing in a kind of suffering sponsorship for the race.

Now the word *vicarious* is chosen to represent and gather up into itself all these varieties of expression. It is the same word, in the root, as the word *vice* in vicegerent, viceroy, vicar-general, vice-president, and the like. It is a word that carries always a face of substitution, indicating that one person comes in place, somehow, of another. Thus a vice-president is one who is to act in certain contingencies, as and for the president; a viceroy, for the king. The ecclesiastical vicar, too, was a vicar as being sent to act for the monastic body, whose duties were laid as a charge upon him; and the pope is called the vicar of Christ, in the same way, as being authorised to fill Christ's place. Any person acts vicariously, in this view, just so far as he comes in place of another. The commercial agent, the trustee, the attorney, are examples of vicarious actions at common law.

Then if we speak of "sacrifice," any person acts in a way of "vicarious sacrifice," not when he burns upon an altar in some other's place, but when he makes loss for him, even as he would make a loss for himself, in the offering of a sacrifice for his sin. The expression is a figure, representing that the party making such sacrifice for another, comes into burden, pain, weariness, or even to the yielding up of life for his sake. The word "vicarious" does not say all, nor the word "sacrifice," but the two together make out the true figure of Christ and His Gospel.

In this sense it is that Christianity or the Christian salvation is a vicarious sacrifice. It does not mean simply that Christ puts Himself into the case of man as a helper; one man helps another without any vicarious relationship implied or supposed. Neither does it mean that Christ undertakes for man in a way of influence; one man tries to influence another, without coming at all into his place. Neither does the vicarious sacrifice imply that He simply comes under common liabilities with us, as when every citizen suffers for the wrongs and general misconduct and consequent misgovernment of the community to which he belongs. Nor that He simply comes into the track of those penal retributions which outrun the wrongs they chastise, passing over upon the innocent, as the sins of fathers propagate their evils in the generations of their children coming after. The idea of Christ's vicarious sacrifice is not matched by any of these lighter examples, though it has something in common with them all, and is therefore just so much likelier to be confounded with them by a lighter and really sophistical interpretation.

On the other hand, we are not to hold the Scripture terms of vicarious sacrifice, as importing a literal substitution of places, by which Christ becomes a sinner for sinners, or penally subject to our deserved penalties. That is a kind of substitution that offends every strongest sentiment of our nature. He cannot become guilty for us. Neither, as God is a just being, can He be anyhow punishable in our place—all God's moral sentiments would be revolted by that. And if Christ should Himself consent to such punishment, He would only ask to have all the most immovable convictions, both of God's moral nature and our own, confounded, or eternally put by.

Excluding now all these under-stated and over-stated explanations, we come to the true conception, which is that Christ, in what is called His vicarious sacrifice, simply engages, at the expense of great suffering and even of death itself, to bring us out of our sins themselves and so out of their penalties; being Himself profoundly identified with us in our fallen state, and burdened in feeling with our evils. Nor is there anything so remote, or difficult, or violent, in this vicarious relation assumed by Christ as many appear to suppose. It would rather be a wonder if, being what He is, He did not assume it. For we are to see and make our due account of this one fact, that a good being is, by the supposition, ready, just according to his goodness, to act vicariously in behalf of any bad or miserable being whose condition he is able to restore. For a good being is not simply one who gives bounties and favours, but one who is in the principle of love; and it is the nature of love, universally, to insert itself into the miseries and take upon its feeling the burdens of others. Love does not consider the ill desert of the subject; he may even be a cruel and relentless enemy. It does not consider the expense of toil, and sacrifice, and suffering the intervention may cost. It stops at nothing but the known impossibility of relief or benefit; asks for nothing as inducement, but the opportunity of success. Love is a principle essentially vicarious in its own nature, identifying the subject with others, so as to suffer their adversities and pains, and taking on itself the burden of their evils. It does not come in officiously and abruptly, and propose to be substituted in some formal and literal way that overturns all the moral relations of law and desert, but it clings to the evil and lost man as in feeling, afflicted for him, burdened by his ill deserts, incapacities, and pains, encountering gladly any loss or suffering for his sake. Approving nothing wrong in him, but faithfully reproving and condemning him in all sin, it is yet made sin—plunged, so to speak, into all the fortunes of sin, by its friendly sympathy. In this manner it is entered vicariously into sacrifice on his account. So naturally and easily does the vicarious sacrifice commend itself to our intelligence, by the stock ideas and feelings out of which it grows.

How it was with Christ, and how He bore our sins, we can see exactly, from a very impressive and remarkable passage in Matthew's Gospel, where he conceives that Christ is entered vicariously into men's diseases, just as He is elsewhere shown to bear, and to be vicariously entered into, the burden of their sins. I produce the passage, at this early point in the discussion, because of the very great and decisive importance it has; for it is remarkable as being the one Scripture citation that gives, beyond a question, the exact *usus loquendi* of all the vicarious and sacrificial language of the New Testament.

Christ has been pouring out His sympathies all day, in acts of healing, run down, as it were, by the wretched multitudes crowding about Him and imploring His pity. No humblest, most repulsive creature is neglected or fails to receive His tenderest, most brotherly consideration. His heart accepts each one as a burden upon its feeling, and by that feeling He is inserted into the lot, the pain, the sickness, the sorrow of each. And so the evangelist, having, as we see, no reference whatever to the substitution for sin, says—"That it might be fulfilled which was spoken by Esaias the prophet, saying—'Himself took our infirmities, and bare our sicknesses.'"* And the text is the more remarkable that the passage he cites from Isaiah, is from his 53rd chapter, which is, in fact, a kind of stock chapter, whence all the most vicarious language of the New Testament is drawn. Besides, the word *bare* occurs in the citation; a word that is based on the very same figure of carrying as that which is used in the expression, "bare our sins," "bare the sins of many," and is moreover precisely the same word which is used by the Apostle when he says "Bear ye one another's burdens, and so fulfil the law of Christ." If then we desire to know exactly what the substitution of Christ for sin was, and how far it went—what it means for example that He bare our sin—we have only to revert back to what is here said of His relation to sicknesses, and our question is resolved.

What does it mean, that Christ "bare our sicknesses"? Does it mean that He literally had our sicknesses transferred to Him, and so taken off

* Matth, viii, 17.

from us? Does it mean that He became blind for the blind, lame for the lame, a leper for the lepers, suffering in Himself all the fevers and pains He took away from others? No one had ever such a thought. How then did He bear our sicknesses, or in what sense? In the sense that He took them on His feeling, had His heart burdened by the sense of them, bore the disgusts of their loathsome decays, felt their pains over again, in the tenderness of His more than human sensibility. Thus manifestly it was that He bare our sicknesses—His very love to us put Him, so far, in a vicarious relation to them, and made Him, so far, a partaker in them.

Here then we have the true law of interpretation, when the vicarious relation of Christ to our sins comes into view. It does not mean that He takes them literally upon Him, as some of the old theologians and a very few moderns appear to believe; it does not mean that He took their ill desert upon Him by some mysterious act of imputation, or had their punishment transferred to His Person. A sickness might possibly be transferred, but a sin cannot by any rational possibility. It does not mean that He literally came into the hell of our retributive evils under sin, and satisfied, by His own suffering, the violated justice of God; for that kind of penal suffering would satisfy nothing but the very worst injustice. No, but the bearing of our sins does mean, that Christ bore them on His feeling, became inserted into their bad lot by His sympathy as a friend, yielded up Himself and His life, even, to an effort of restoring mercy; in a word, that He bore our sins in just the same sense that He bore our sicknesses. Understand that love itself is an essentially vicarious principle, and the solution is no longer difficult.

See how it is with love in the case of a mother. She loves her child, and it comes out in that fact, or from it, that she watches for the child, bears all its pains and sicknesses on her own feeling, and when it is wronged, is stung herself, by the wrong put upon it, more bitterly far than the child. She takes every chance of sacrifice for it, as her own opportunity. She creates, in fact, imaginary ills for it, because she has not opportunities enough of sacrifice. In the same manner a friend that is real and true takes all the sufferings, losses, wrongs, indignities, of a friend on his own feeling, and will sometimes suffer more for him than he does for himself. So also with the patriot or citizen who truly loves his country, even though that love is mixed with many false fires that are only fires of ambition or revenge—how does it wrench his feeling, what a burden does it lay upon his concern, by day and by night, when that country, so dear to him, is being torn by faction, and the fate of its laws and liberties is thrown upon the chances of an armed rebellion. Then you will see how many thousands of citizens, who never knew before what sacrifices it was in the power of their love to make for their country's welfare, rush to the field and throw their bodies and dear lives on the battle's edge to save it!

Thus it is that every sort of love is found twining its feeling always into the feeling, and loss, and want, and woe, of whatever people, or person, or even enemy, it loves; thus that God Himself takes our sinning enmity upon His heart, painfully burdened by our broken state, and travailing, in all the deepest feeling of His nature, to recover us to Himself. And this it is which the cross and vicarious sacrifice of Jesus signify to us, or outwardly express. Such a God in love, must be such a Saviour in suffering—He could not well be other or less. There is a Gethsemane hid in all love, and when the fit occasion comes, no matter how great and high the subject may be, its heavy groaning will be heard—even as it was in Christ. He was in an agony, exceeding sorrowful even unto death. By that sign it was that God's love broke into the world, and Christianity was born!

Here, then, as I conceive, is the true seed-principle of the Christian salvation. What we call the vicarious sacrifice of Christ is nothing strange as regards the principle of it, no superlative, unexampled, and therefore unintelligible grace. It only does and suffers, and comes into substitution for, just what any and all love will, according to its degree. And, in this view, it is not something higher in principle than our human virtue knows, and which we ourselves are never to copy or receive, but it is to be understood by what we know already, and is to be more fully understood by what we are to know hereafter, when we are complete in Christ. Nothing is wanting to resolve the vicarious sacrifice of Jesus, but the commonly known, always familiar principle of love accepted as the fundamental law of duty, even by mankind. Given the universality of love, the universality of vicarious sacrifice is given also. Here is the centre and deepest spot of good, or goodness, conceivable. At this point we look into heaven's eye itself, and read the meaning of all heavenly grace.*

---

* [Ed.] For an interesting criticism of Bushnell's interpretation of vicarious atonement, see Henry James, Sr.'s review of *The Vicarious Sacrifice*, published in the *North American Review*, CII (April 1866), pp. 556–71. James attacked Bushnell's theory by questioning the psychological analogy on which the above passage is based. Human love, said James, simply does not have the vicarious or self-sacrificing quality that Bushnell attributed to it.

# From "Our Gospel a Gift to the Imagination" (1869)*

[The Christian gospel] offers itself first of all and principally to the interpretative imaginings and discernings of faith, never, save in that manner, to the constructive processes of logic and speculative opinion. It is, in one sense, pictorial; its every line or lineament is traced in some image or metaphor, and by no possible ingenuity can it be gotten away from metaphor; for as certainly as one metaphoric image is escaped by a definition, another will be taken up, and must be, to fill its place in the definition itself. Mathematical language is a scheme of exact notation. All words that are names of mere physical acts and objects are literal, and even animals can, so far, learn their own names and the meaning of many acts done or commanded. But no animal ever understood a metaphor: that belongs to intelligence, and to man as a creature of intelligence; being a power to see, in all images, the faces of truth, and take their sense, or read [intus lego] their meaning, when thrown up in language before the imagination.

Every word is a figure called in to serve a metaphoric use, in virtue of the fact that it has a physical base naturally significant of the spiritual truth or meaning it is used metaphorically to express. Physical bases are timber, in this manner, of all mental language, and are generally traced in the etymologies of the dictionaries; though sometimes they are lost and cannot be traced. And it is not merely the verbs, nouns, adjectives, that carry these metaphoric uses, but their very grammar of relationship, is also framed in terms of space by the little words called prepositions, which show their spatial images in their faces, up, down, by, through, to, under, from, beyond and the like. The whole web of speech is curiously woven metaphor, and we are able to talk out our thoughts in it,—never one of them visible,—by throwing out metaphoric images in metaphoric grammar so as to give them expression.

Let us go back now and take our lesson at the type history of the Scriptures. The temple and the whole temple service,—the sacrifices, lustrations of blood, purifyings, and the like,—was a figure, an apostle declares, for the time then present. His word here is parabole [parable.] Sometimes he uses the word image, sometimes ensample, and oftener

* [Ed.] Hours at Home, X (December 1869), pp. 159–72. Republished in Building Eras in Religion (New York: Charles Scribner's Sons, 1881), pp. 249–85. Included here, from Building Eras: pp. 252–56, 261–63.

the word *type*; but they all mean nearly the same thing. And here it is that we come upon the curiously fantastic type-learning, which figures so conspicuously in the sermons, commentaries, and theologic treatises of the former time. It is only fit subject of mirth, when it assumes that the types were given to signify to the ages that received them the great living truths of Christianity, and not to be vehicle and metaphor, afterward, for them when they should arrive. These types, patterns, shadows, images, parables, ensamples, or whatever else they were called, are simply bases of words prepared to serve as metaphors of the new salvation when it should come. And for this purpose, in part, the altar service was instituted; for the gospel grace was to be a grace supernatural, and there were no types, no bases of words in nature, that could serve the necessary metaphoric uses. All the natural metaphors were in a lower field of significance, and all mere natural language fell short of the mark. . . .

But we must look into language itself and see how the great revelation of God is coming and to come. First of all, it is impossible, as we have seen already that any terms of language for mental notions, things of the spirit, unseen worlds, beings invisible, should ever exist, save as there are physical images found to serve as metaphoric bases of the necessary words; for we cannot show them to the eye and then name them, as we do acts or objects visible; we can only hint them by figures, or objects metaphorically significant of them. And so we see beforehand, that all the truths of religion are going to be given to men by images; so that all God's truth will come as to the imagination. Hence the necessity of the old physical religion to prepare draperies and figures for the new. Hence also, when we come to the new, we are constantly met, we perhaps know not why or how, by images taken from the old, in a way that seems half fanciful and curiously mystical. Adam is the figure of him that was to come, the second Adam, because he, Christ, was to be the head, correspondently, of a spiritual generation. Christ is David, Melchizedek, high priest, the spiritual Rock, a prophet like unto Moses and I know not what beside. John the Baptist is Elias that was to come. In the same manner, heaven is a paradise or garden, or a new Jerusalem, or a state of glorious city life in God; the new society of grace is to be the kingdom of God, or the kingdom of heaven; and Christ himself is Messiah, that is, king. All the past is taken up as metaphor for all the future. All these things, we are to say, "happened unto them for ensamples," that is, types for the expression of our higher truth.

And so we are questioning often about the credibility of a double meaning in scripture; as if it were a thing fanciful beyond belief. Whereas the meanings double and redouble as often as new typologies are made ready. The spiritual comes out of the physical, and the more spiritual out of the less; just because one thing is ready for the expression of another and still another. There is nothing fantastical in it, but it comes to pass under a fixed law of language,—all language, even the most common,—even as a stalk of corn pushes out leaf from within leaf by a growth that is its unsheathing.

Every dictionary shows the unsheathing process always going on; meanings coming out of meanings, and second senses doubling upon first, and third upon second, and so every symbol breeding families of meanings on to the tenth or twentieth and saying always, in the scripture way: "that so it might be fulfilled." This fulfilling is no scripture conceit, but is the systematic fact of language itself. . . .

[This law of language is apparent in] the great reconciliation or atonement, in Christ's life and death. Plainly there was here no lamb, no fire, no altar, no literal sacrifice. There was a blood of murder, but no rite in blood, no sprinkling, no kind of lustral ceremony. And yet all these things are here as in metaphor, and are meant to be. One great object of the old ritual was to prepare these images and get them ready as a higher language for the supernatural truth. The people of the law were put in training under these patterns of the heavenly things, till the very mind of their nation should be stocked with images and metaphors thence derived for the heavenly things themselves. Who could ever have conceived the ministry and death of Jesus in these words of atonement, sacrifice, and cleansing, whose mind had not first been Judaized in the stock images of its thinking? Suppose, for example, that some gifted Greek, having a soul configured to Plato's methods and ideas, had been with Christ, as Peter was, all through his life, and then, after his death, had written his epistle to expound him and his religion to the world. What could he have said of him more adequate than to set him forth as a beautiful and wise character doing wonders by his power; a friend of the poor, a healer of the sick, patient of contradiction, submissive to enemies, meek, true, the ever good, the perfect fair? That he has done any thing which can be called his sacrifice, any thing to recompose the breach of sin or to reconcile the world to God, will not occur to him, and he has no words to speak of any such thing. Not one matter most distinctively prominent in Christ's work, as expounded by his apostles, filling out in metaphoric glory all the terms of the altar, could have been given, or even thought by him. All the better, many will now say; we shall gladly be rid of all such altar figures; for it is too late in the day to be making Hebrews of us now. But suppose it should happen to be true that the all-wise God made Hebrews partly for this very thing, to bring figures into speech that Greeks and Saxons had not; that so he might give to the world the perfectly transcendent, supernatural matter of a grace that reaches high enough to cover and compose the relations of men to his government, a grace of reconciliation. Call the words "old clothes" then

of the Hebrews,° putting what contempt we may upon them, still they
are such types and metaphors of God's mercy as he has been able to
prepare, and Christ is in them as in "glorious apparel!" Why to say:
"Behold the Lamb of God, that taketh away the sin of the world," signifies, in the heart's uses, more than whole volumes of palaver in any possible words of natural language. No living disciple, having once gotten the
sense of these types of the altar, will ever try to get his gospel out of
them and preach it in the common terms of language. Quite as certainly
will he never try, having once gotten their meaning, to hold them
literally,—Christ made literally sin for us, a literal Lamb, literal sacrifice,
bleeding literally for the uses of his blood. But he will want them as the
dear interpreters and equivalents of God's mercy in the cross, putting
himself before them to read and read again, and drink and drink again
their full divine meanings into his soul. Beholding more truths in their
faces than all the contrived theories and speculated propositions of
schools, he will stay fast by them, or in them, wanting never to get clear
of them, or away from the dear and still more dear impression of their
power.

° [Ed.] Thomas Carlyle, in *Sartor Resartus* (1833–1834), referred to Biblical imagery as
"Hebrew old clothes."

# PART III

# SOCIAL STUDIES

# SOCIAL STUDIES

Power moves in the direction of hope.
                    —Bushnell, "The Growth of Law"

Bushnell's faith in the power of Christian character to communicate itself through the organic channels of social life sometimes gave his commentary on American society a cloyingly optimistic cast, but never completely deprived it of a critical edge. On the one hand, he pinned his hopes to the belief that the good middle-class American citizens he knew were tolerable representatives of ideal Christian character, and therefore that the spread of American culture could be equated with the "Christianization" of the world. Our character, he might have said, insures and justifies our manifest destiny. On the other hand, he was sensitive to forces in America that threatened to destroy the unities of culture, and therefore to disrupt the organic channels of community life through which the work of Christianization was supposedly being accomplished. In an age when individualism was common sense, Bushnell stood for the virtues of tradition and organic community.

"The True Wealth or Weal of Nations" (1837) is an early expression of Bushnell's confidence in American destiny. This rather extravagant eulogy comes complete with references to the genetic superiority of the British stock and the redemptive influences of the American landscape—all fairly typical of the utopian-jingoist oratory of his day. In similarly lavish rhetoric, "Barbarism the First Danger" (1837) presents a darker side of this same vision, expressing Bushnell's fear of what might happen to American moral standards as more and more settlers moved to the West. Like de Crevecoeur, he associated the raw wilderness with barbarism, and like many preachers of his time, he called for religious missions to win settlers back to civilized ways. (The passages on slavery in this address, together with the conclusion to "Our Obligation to the Dead," present a fair summary of Bushnell's critique of that institution and a fair indication of his limitations on the question.) In spite of his alarm over certain trends in American culture, however, Bushnell proved to be an optimist at last. "How to Be a Christian in Trade" (1872) asserts his confidence that the general drift of American society—the business establishment included—was towards the ever move complete "Christianization" of culture.

As we have already noted, the Christianization of society, like that of individuals, is a process supposedly carried forward by the force of individual character expressing itself through the organic channels of society. In *Women's Suffrage; The Reform Against Nature* (1869), Bushnell gives an estimate of the role of women in this process. As a spokesman for the nineteenth century's "cult of true womanhood," he insists that women are the primary purveyors of the subtle magnetism or "influence" of character in a wicked world. This is their glory as Christians; it is also their limit as social beings, since, as Bushnell goes on to argue, women can not assume "men's roles" without losing the influence proper to them and necessary to the well-being of Christian culture.

Finally, "Our Obligations to the Dead" (1865) expresses Bushnell's hope that the elusive organic unity of American society—the necessary groundwork for the triumph of Christian character—may have been established once and for all through the common suffering of the nation in the Civil War. As the suffering and bloodshed of Christ on the cross prepared the power of influence that created Christendom, so perhaps the bloodshed of the American dead has prepared a new national life, a new literature, and a more profound sense of community. In this address—a declaration of America's cultural independence in the lineage of Emerson's "American Scholar"—Bushnell's interpretation of the nature and function of Christianity fuses with his vision of the American future.

# From "The True Wealth or Weal of Nations" (1837)*

There are too many prophetic signs admonishing us that almighty Providence is preengaged to make this a truly great nation, not to be cheered by them and set ourselves to search after the true principles of national welfare with a confidence that here at last they are to find their opportunity. This western world had not been preserved unknown through so many ages for any purpose less sublime than to be opened at a certain stage of history, and to become the theater wherein better principles might have room and free development. Out of all the inhabitants of the world, too, a select stock, the Saxon, and out of this the British family, the noblest of the stock, was chosen to people our country, that our eagle, like that of the prophet, might have the cedars of Lebanon and the topmost branches of the cedars to plant by his great waters.† A belt of temperate climate was also marked out for our country in the midst of a vast continent, with a view, it would seem, to preserve the vigor of the stock and make it fruitful here, as it ever has been, in great names and great actions. Furthermore, it is impossible to glance at the very singular territory we occupy, without perceiving that the two great elements of force are to be developed together in this people as they never yet have been in history. These elements of course are weight and motion,—vastness of conception and vigor of action. Though we have a field every way ample to contain two hundred millions of inhabitants, there is yet no vast central inland remote from the knowledge and commerce of mankind, where a people may dream out life in the gigantic, but crude and sluggish images of Asiatic repose. Vast as it is and filling the minds of its people always with images of vastness, it is yet surrounded like the British islands and permeated like Venice itself by the waters of commerce—becoming thus a field of vastness not in repose, but in action. On the west it meets the Pacific and the waters of another hemisphere. On the east and south a long bold line of coast sweeps round, showing the people more than a thousand leagues of the highway

* [Ed.] Originally presented as a Phi Beta Kappa oration at Yale and published in pamphlet form as *On the Principles of National Greatness*. Republished under the present title in *Work and Play* (New York: Charles Scribner, 1864), pp. 43–77. Included here, from *Work and Play*: pp. 45–47, 76–77.

† [Ed.] On the theme of Saxon racial superiority, see also *Christian Nurture* (New York: Charles Scribner, 1861), Ch. 8: "The Out-Populating Power of the Christian Stock."

of the world. On the north, again, stretches a vast mediterranean of congregated seas, sounding to each other in a boisterous wild chorus, and opening their gates to the commerce of far distant regions. Then again, across the land, down all the slopes and through valleys large enough for empires, sweep rivers that are moving lakes. All the features of the land are such as conspire to form a people of vast conceptions and the most intense practical vigor and activity. And already do these two elements of force appear in our people in a combination more striking and distinct than ever before in any people whose education was so unripe. Need I say that such a people cannot exist without a great history? We have been told that stars of nobility and orders of hierarchy, as they exist in the old world, are indispensable as symbols to make authority visible and inspire the people with great and patriotic sentiments. But how shall we long for these in a country where God has ennobled the land itself in every feature, filling it with the signs of his own august royalty, and training the people up to spiritual vastness and force by symbols of his own! . . .

I see the nation rising from its present depression with a chastened, but good spirit.* I see education beginning to awake, a spirit of sobriety ruling in business and in manners, religion animated in her heavenly work, a higher self-respect invigorating our institutions, and the bonds of our country strengthened by a holier attachment. Our eagle ascends and spreads his wings abroad from the eastern to the western ocean. A hundred millions of intelligent and just people dwell in his shadow. Churches are sprinkled throughout the whole field. The sabbath sends up its holy voice. The seats of philosophers and poets are distinguished in every part, and hallowed by the affections of the people. The fields smile with agriculture. The streams and lakes and all the waters of the world bear the riches of their commerce. The people are elevated in stature, both mental and bodily; they are happy, orderly, brave and just, and the world admires one true example of greatness in a people.

* [Ed.] A reference to the nationwide economic crisis of 1837.

# From "Barbarism the First Danger" (1847)*

Nothing is more certain . . . than that *emigration or a new settlement of the social state involves a tendency to social decline.* There must in every such case be a relapse toward barbarism, more or less protracted, more or less complete. Commonly nothing but extraordinary efforts in behalf of education and religion will suffice to prevent a fatal lapse of social order. Apart from this great truth, clearly seen as enveloped in the practical struggles of our American history, no one can understand its real import, the problem it involves or the position at which we have now arrived. Least of all can he understand the sublime relation of home missions and other like enterprises to the unknown future of our great nation. He must know that we are a people trying out the perils incident to a new settlement of the social state; he must behold religion passing out into the wilds of nature with us to fortify law, industry and good manners, and to bear up our otherwise declining fortunes till we become an established and fully cultivated people. Just here hang all the struggles of our history for the two centuries now past, and for at least another century to come.

We shall also discover in pursuing our subject, in what manner we are to apprehend danger from the spread of Romanism.† If you seem to struggle in this matter of Romanism with contrary convictions; to see reason in the alarms urged upon you so frequently, and yet feel it to be the greatest unreason to fear the prevalence here of a religion so distinctively opposite to our character and institutions; if you are half frighted by the cry of Romanism, and half scorn it as a bugbear, you will be able to settle yourself into a sober and fixed opinion of the subject when you perceive that we are in danger, first, of something far worse than Romanism and through that of Romanism itself. OUR FIRST DANGER

* [Ed.] An oration delivered in New York, Boston, and elsewhere in May and June of 1847. This address won Bushnell his first wide-spread fame. Published in the 1881 edition of *Work and Play* (New York: Charles Scribner's Sons, 1881), pp. 227–67, and in subsequent editions of the same work. Included here: pp. 229–33, 248–67.

† [Ed.] Bushnell is referring to popular fears that there was a secret Roman Catholic conspiracy to take over the Mississippi River Valley—a fear fueled by books such as Lyman Becher's *A Plea for the West* (1832). On the prevalence of anti-Roman Catholic or "Nativist" sentiment in early nineteenth century America, see Ray Allen Billington, *The Protestant Crusade, 1800–1860* (New York: 1938; rpt. Chicago: Quadrangle Books, 1964).

IS BARBARISM—Romanism next; for before we can think it a religion
to have a Levite to our priest, we must bring back the times of the
Judges. Let us empty ourselves of our character, let us fall into superstition through the ignorance, wildness and social confusion incident to a
migratory habit and a rapid succession of new settlements, and Romanism will find us just where character leaves us. The real danger is the
prior. Taking care of that we are safe. Sleeping over that, nothing ought
to save us; for if we must have a wild race of nomads roaming over the
vast western territories of our land—a race without education, law,
manners or religion—we need not trouble ourselves farther on account
of Romanism, for to such a people Romanism, bad as it is, will come as a
blessing.

I shall recur to this question of Romanism again. I only name it here
as a preliminary that may assist you to apprehend the true import of my
subject. Let us now proceed to the question itself, How far emigration
and a continual resettlement, as in this country, involves a tendency to
moral and social disorganization? In the discussion of this question I shall
draw principally on the facts of history; I only suggest here, as a pre-
parative and key to the facts that may be cited, a few of the reasons why
such a decline is likely to appear.

First of all, the society transplanted in a case of emigration cannot
carry its roots with it; for society is a vital creature, having roots of
antiquity which inhere in the very soil, in the spots consecrated by valor,
by genius and by religion. Transplanted to a new field, the emigrant
race lose, of necessity, a considerable portion of that vital force which is
the organific and conserving power of society. All the old roots of local
love and historic feeling, the joints and bands that minister nourishment,
are left behind; and nothing remains to organize a living growth but the
two unimportant incidents, proximity and a common interest.

Education must for a long time be imperfect in degree and partial
in extent. There is no literary atmosphere breathing through the forests
or across the prairies. The colleges, if any they have, are only rudimental
beginnings, and the youth a raw company of woodsmen. Hurried into
life at the bar or in the pulpit when as yet they are only half-educated,
their performances are crude in the matter and rough in the form. No
matter how cultivated the professional men of the first age, those of the
second, third and fourth will mix up extravagance and cant in all their
demonstrations, and will be acceptable to the people partly for that
reason. For the immense labors and rough hardships necessary to be
encountered in the way of providing the means of living will ordinarily
create in them a rough and partially wild habit.

Then, as their tastes grow wild, their resentments will grow violent
and their enjoyments coarse. The salutary restraints of society being to a

great extent removed, they will think it no degradation to do before the woods and wild animals what in the presence of a cultivated social state they would blush to perpetrate. They are likely even to look upon the indulgence of low vices and brutal pleasures as the necessary garnish of their life of adventure.

In religion, their views will of course be narrow and crude and their animosities bitter. Sometimes the very life of religion will seem about to die, as it actually would, save that some occasional outburst of over-wrought feeling or fanatical zeal kindles a temporary fire. Probably it will be found that low superstitions begin to creep in, a regarding of dreams, a faith in the presentation of Scripture texts, in apparitions and visions, perhaps also in necromancy. . . .*

[Finally,] a considerable portion of the new West has a social and historical connection with slavery which is continually doubling the inherent perils of emigration itself.

And here, since this institution of slavery entering into the fortunes of our history complicates in so many ways the disorders we suffer, I must pause a few moments to sketch its characteristics. Slavery, it is not to be denied, is an essentially barbarous institution. It gives us too that sign which is the perpetual distinction of barbarism, that it has no law of progress. The highest level it reaches is the level at which it begins. Indeed, we need not scruple to allow that it has yielded us one consider-able advantage in virtue of the fact that it produces its best condition first. For while the northern people were generally delving in labor for many generations to create a condition of comfort, slavery set the mas-ters at once on a footing of ease, gave them leisure for elegant inter-course or unprofessional studies, and seasoned their character thus with that kind of cultivation which distinguishes men of society. A class of statesmen were thus raised up who were prepared to figure as leaders in scenes of public life, where so much depends on manners and social address. But now the scale is changing. Free labor is rising at length into a state of wealth and comfort, to take the lead of American society. Meanwhile, the foster sons of slavery—the high families, the statesmen—gradually receding in character as they must under this vicious institu-tion, are receding also in power and influence and have been ever since the revolution. Slavery is a condition against nature; the curse of nature therefore is on it, and it bows to its doom by a law as irresistible as grav-ity. It produces a condition of ease which is not the reward of labor, and a state of degradation which is not the curse of idleness. Therefore the

---

* [Ed.] A reference to the excesses of frontier revivalism, and to the West as a breeding ground for radical sectarian movements. For an analysis of the phenomena Bushnell had in mind here, see Whitney R. Cross, *The Burned-Over District* (Ithaca: Cornell Univer-sity Press, 1950).

ease it enjoys cannot but end in a curse, and the degradation it suffers cannot rise into a blessing. It nourishes imperious and violent passions. It makes the masters solitary sheiks on their estates, forbidding thus the possibility of public schools, and preventing also that condensed form of society which is necessary to the vigorous maintenance of churches. . . .

Connected with this moral decay, the resources of nature also are exhausted and her fertile territories changed to a desert by the uncreating power of a spendthrift institution. And then, having made a waste where God had made a garden, slavery gathers up the relics of bankruptcy and the baser relics still of virtue and all manly enterprise, and goes forth to renew on a virgin soil its dismal and forlorn history. Thus, at length, has been produced what may be called the bowie-knife style of civilization, and the new Southwest is overrun by it: a spirit of blood which defies all laws of God and man; honorable but not honest; prompt to resent an injury, slack to discharge a debt; educated to ease, and readier of course when the means of living fail to find them at the gambling-table or the race-ground than in any work of industry, probably squandering the means of living there to relieve the tedium of ease itself.

Such is the influence of slavery, as it enters into our American social state, and imparts its moral type of barbarism through emigration to the new West. Hence the Mexican war, which has its beginning and birth in what I have called the bowie-knife style of civilization—a war in the nineteenth century which, if not begun for that purpose, many are visibly determined shall be a war for the extension of slavery. It was no one political party, as some pretend, who made this war, but it was the whole Southwest and West rather of all parties,* instigated by a wild and riotous spirit of adventure which no terms of reason or of Christian prudence and humanity could check. And if this war results as probably it may in the acquisition of a vast western territory, then is our great pasture-ground of barbarism so much to be enlarged, the room to run wild extended, the chances of final anarchy and confusion multiplied.

We are now prepared to complete our view by passing directly to the subject of western emigration itself. And what are the moral and social results here preparing? . . .

Western character has many powerful and promising qualities, but it wants the salt of religious virtue, the sobriety of discipline and the modesty of true intelligence. It is frank, bold, earnest and positive, but somewhat rude and extravagant, and specially destitute of the genial sentiments which enrich the more settled and cultivated forms of society. A very large portion of the western community, it is well known, are already so far gone

---

* [Ed.] The desire of slave-holding states to expand the territory open to slavery is frequently cited as a cause of the Mexican War. On the whole, Democrats sided with southern interests, while Whigs condemned the war.

in ignorance as to make a pride of it, and even to decry education as an over-genteel accomplishment. They hold of course their manhood in their will, not in their understanding; which is the same as to say that law is weak and passion violent. Hence the many public murders committed in the newer states of the West and South, which are never legally investigated. Or perhaps you will even see an ambitious young city mustering itself in a military mob to murder an inoffensive Christian minister and citizen; and when it is done, when the fit of passion is over, the law, instead of rising up to reassert its rights as we see it do in older and less barbarous communities, still sleeping in its violated majesty. Or, if you will discover how near it is possible to come and within how short a time to a complete dissolution of civil order, you may see the executive power of a sovereign state standing by for six months to look on as a spectator, while two organized military parties of its own citizens are prosecuting an open way, one to defend, the other to capture, an American city!* Where shall such disorders stop? and what is the limit toward which they run? If in the days of the Judges Pennsylvania rebelled against the excise of whisky, and now Illinois substitutes the camp and the siege in place of justice itself and the ordinary methods of legal redress, what shall by and by appear in some new state as far west of Illinois as that is of Pennsylvania? What are we to expect as this reign of passion, spreading onward across the vast regions yet unoccupied, grows yet more violent as it is deeper in ignorance, and wilder still as it is more remote from the haunts of Christian civilization? Is it not well understood that a partially wild race of men, such as cannot any longer be properly included in terms of civilization, is already formed? I speak of what is sometimes called the pioneer race. They roll on like a prairie fire before the advance of regular emigration; they have no fixed habits and do not care to appropriate the soil, consequently have no education or religion. They live mainly by hunting and pasture; and when a regular settlement is begun within an hour's ride they feel proximity too close, quit their hut of logs, which is in fact only their tent, and start on by another long remove into the wild regions beyond them. These semibarbarians too are continually multiplying in numbers and becoming more distinct in their habits. Erelong, there is reason to fear, they will be scouring in populous bands over the vast territories of Oregon and California, to be known as the pasturing tribes, the wild hunters and robber clans of the western hemisphere— American Moabites, Arabs and Edomites! . . .

Enough that we understand the magnificence of the problem, and the tremendous perils incident thereto: that we have it on hand to struggle up for a half century to come against the downward currents of

---

* [Ed.] Probably a reference to a series of clashes between two *ad hoc* citizens' armies, the "Regulators" and the "Flatheads," in Massac County, Illinois, widely publicized throughout the 1840s.

decline, and bear up the nation with us into a settled condition of Christian culture and virtue; which if we do, the critical point of our destiny is turned. We are then to be the most august and happiest nation that has ever appeared on earth, the leading power of the world's history. Was there ever a struggle offered to the good and great of mankind so fit to kindle enthusiasm or nerve the soul to patient sacrifices! What then shall we do?

First of all, we must not despair. There is no cause for despair. Dark as the picture is that I have given, I do not for one suffer a misgiving thought. In many portions of the field the crisis is already past. In others it soon will be. And every new state or section added to the parts already secure brings an accession of aid and a more preponderant weight of influence. Of the new regions, we may say that Vermont, Western New York and part of Ohio are already gained and are now side by side with us, helping us to support the downward pressure of the emigrant masses. We have only to make sure, in like manner, of all the States this side of the Mississippi, and then the critical point is in my estimation past. Much will remain to be done, but the result will be sure. For when once the vast region this side of the Mississippi is seen to be ascending with us into order and Christian refinement, the regions beyond will scarcely be able to draft themselves down into anarchy. The die of our destiny is cast. Seeing then the momentous perils that hang about us, let them only quicken us to a more fixed and heroic devotion. It must be a faint heart that cannot bear up in a struggle so evidently temporary. Nothing is more certain than that if we deserve to triumph we shall triumph; and if that be not enough to sustain our courage we are worthy of no such cause as this.

Besides, we are not to forget our advantage under what may be called the new dispensation of railroads and telegraphs; for by these, spinning out into the new regions, spaces are annihilated and all parts of the nation, new and old, are kept in such proximity as to vary all the former incidents of emigration. In one view there is no emigration left. Minnesota and Oregon are here at Boston, and here at New York, Philadelphia, Hartford, touched by all the refinements, principles, high sentiments of society, held in the juxtaposition even of a present feeling. Now, therefore, is the time for nations to be born in a day, for by a wonderful celerity of progress every new community ripens into age and character almost as soon as the ink of its patents or land-title records is dry.*

But we have more to do than to be looking after either courage or encouragements—something to be promptly and bravely done, done

---

* [Ed.] For a more extensive celebration of the civilizing power of new communications technologies, see "The Day of Roads," *Work and Play* (New York: Charles Scribner, 1864), pp. 409–445.

with a resolute fidelity and a thorough devotion to the Christian future of the country. I cannot here find room to enlarge on what does not belong to the occasion for which I speak. Suffice it to say that we have great works of education to foster, and foundations of learning to lay for the generations to come; the ferocity of party politics to soften or civilize, subjecting, if possible, the coarse animosities and rude barbarities of political strife to the moderating power of candor, courtesy and a genuine public spirit; slavery to grapple with by that wisely moderated, steady maintenance of principle and that sober and lofty statesmanship which are requisite in managing the worst and most formidable of all our social evils, an evil that begins with an essentially barbaric institution and begets some tendency to barbarism in every people infected by its influence.

But the great main hope is in that power which masters all these other modes and means of good, namely: religion. To this let us come directly, and especially to that great cause which undertakes to propagate religion by sending forth a qualified ministry into all the newly settled regions of our great country—the cause, I mean, of home missions.

In no form of human society is there any law of self-support and self-conservation. There is no shape of society, least of all any shape of new society, that will not rot itself down and dissolve, unless there descend upon it from above a conserving power which it has not in itself. Nothing but religion, a ligature binding society to God, can save it. No light save that which is celestial, no virtue but that which is born of God, no power of motivity but that which is drawn from other worlds, can suffice to preserve, compact and edify a new social state. . . .

It is time also to understand that if we are to fill this great field with Christian churches and a Christian people we must have a spirit of life in our breasts, and a tone of Christian devotion such as we have not hitherto exhibited. Here is the only real cause of discouragement I know. It is not money, it is not men, it is no mere human outlay that can bear up such a work as this. We want the unworldly spirit; that which knits us, and through us knits our great country to God. And then also, we want that intense and Christ-like humanity which will attract the feeling of our whole country toward us. For it is not in oppositions, it is not in raising a crusade against Romanism or filling the air with outcries of any sort that we are to save our country. We must rise upon it as the morning in the tranquillity of love. We must rain righteousness upon it as a genial shower.

It is beautiful also to see that God designs by the very work we undertake to fill out and finish our own Christian type of character and society. In the case of our fathers, it seems probable that nothing but the strong pillars of high Calvinism held them up or could have held them up till the critical point of their history was passed. There were no missionaries coming over unto them. Nothing could hold them up but an internal force such as they had in these doctrines—doctrines that were incorporated in their souls as the spinal column in their bodies. Thus, when their manners were grown wild, their sentiments coarse, and their ill-trained understandings generally incapable of nice speculation, still the tough questions of their theology kept them always in action; still they could grasp hold of the great iron pillars of election, reprobation and decrees, and their clumsy-handed thoughts were able to feel them distinctly. Whoever could distinguish a thunderbolt could surely think of these, and it mattered not so much whether they thought exactly aright as that they kept thinking, and in their thinking brought down God upon their souls. So they took hold of the iron pillars that held up the theologic heavens, and climbed and heaved in huge surges of might and kept their gross faculties in exercise, till the critical hour of their trial was passed. The themes they handled kept them before God. They dwelt in the summits of divine government. They looked upon the throne, they heard the thunders roll below and felt the empyrean shake above at the going forth of God's decrees. Such a religion as they had could not be distant or feeble. It had power to invest the coarse mind with a divine presence, and make Jehovah felt as an element of experience. Never was there a better foundation for a grand, massive character in religion; and now God means to finish out this character by uniting in it the softer shades of feeling and the broader compass of a more Catholic and genial spirit. We go forth now to a people who unite all manner of opinions, and we go in company with Christians of other names and other creeds who are undertakers also in the same great work. We cannot, therefore, spend our strength now upon exclusive and distinctive dogmas, but we must proceed in a Catholic and comprehensive spirit. Otherwise we shall be at war with each other, and shall only spend our force in demolishing all the force we have. Thus the Methodists for example have a ministry admirably adapted, as regards their mode of action, to the new West—a kind of light artillery that God has organized to pursue and overtake the fugitives that flee into the wilderness from his presence. They are prompt and effective in action, ready for all service and omnipresent, as it were, in the field. The new settler reaches the ground to be occupied and by the next week he is likely to find the circuit crossing by his door and to hear the voice of one crying in the wilderness: "The kingdom of God is come nigh unto you! . . ." Therefore, let there be if possible no controversy with them; but let us rather encourage ourselves in a work so vast by the fact that we have so vast an army of helpers in the field with us. So of all the other Christian families, who are going into the field to do a work for their Master. There should be not only concord of spirit, but also an actual understanding; so that we may cover together as much ground as possible. And then we should all go forth together to calm the angry divisions of controversy and sweeten the bitter prejudices of sectarian strife. Earnest for the truth, we must also remember that truth itself is Catholic and comprehensive. We must shun that vapid liberalism, which instead of attracting us into unity will only dissolve us into indifference, and yet we must be willing to stretch our forbearance and charity even to Romanists themselves when we clearly find the spirit of Jesus in their life. In this manner God will instruct us by our work, and make our work itself our reward. Engaging with our utmost ardor to save the wilder portions of our country, we shall carry on thus our own noble beginnings to completion, and finish out a character as earnest in its sacrifices and catholic in its charities as it is firm in its original elements. May we not also hope to draw down from the skies upon us and upon all the regions for which we labor such a baptism of love, as will melt both us and them and all the families of Christ in our land into one Christian fraternity?

Thus will we go on and give it to our sons and daughters to come after us. We will measure our strength by the grandeur of our object. The wilderness shall bud and blossom as the rose before us; and we will not cease, till a Christian nation throws up its temples of worship on every hill and plain; till knowledge, virtue and religion, blending their dignity and their healthful power, have filled our great country with a manly and a happy race of people, and the bands of a complete Christian commonwealth are seen to span the continent.

# From "How To Be a Christian in Trade" (1872)*

[It is a] very great moral advantage of trade, that it is just the calling in which a christian man will best learn the uses of money. . . . Hence, I conceive, it is going to be discovered, that the great problem we have now on hand, viz., the christianizing of the money power of the world, depends for its principal hope, on the trading class in society. Talent has been christianized already on a large scale. The political power of states and kingdoms has been long assumed to be, and now at least really is, as far as it becomes their accepted office to maintain personal security and liberty. Architecture, arts, constitutions, schools, and learning, have been largely christianized.† But the money power, which is one of the most operative and grandest of all, is only beginning to be, though with promising tokens of a finally complete reduction to Christ and the uses of his kingdom. In our late civil war, the money power, for the first time, so far as I know, since the world began, laid itself fairly on the altar, and gave itself, in a heartily-pledged devotion, to the public welfare. It even took up, we may say, the nation's heavy and huge bulk, and bore it grandly through on its Atlantean shoulders. Every thing we have for public love, was the maxim even of money, and there was never before a fiscal campaign to match the sublimity and true majesty of the specta- cle. It was the money power standing sponsor for the nation, in its terri- ble baptism of blood. Now what we wait for, and are looking hopefully to see, is a like consecration of the vast money power of the world, to the work, and cause, and kingdom, of Jesus Christ. For that day, when it comes, is the morning, so to speak, of the new creation. That tide-wave in the money power can as little be resisted, when God brings it on, as the tides of the sea; and like these also it will flow across the world in a day. And such a result, I conceive, we are to look for largely, to the merchant class of disciples. Trade expanding into commerce, and com- merce rising into communion, are to be the outline of the story. When

* [Ed.] From *Sermons on Living Subjects* (New York: Scribner, Armstrong & Co., 1872), pp. 243–67. Included here: pp. 263–67.
† [Ed.] Bushnell's idea of a "Christianized" society became a theme of the social gospel movement. Josiah Strong quoted this passage in the chapter titled "Money and the King- dom" in *Our Country* (1885). Walter Rauschenbusch embraced the term in his interpreta- tion of the Kingdom of God as a "Christianized" form of human society—e.g., in *The Christianization of the Social Order* (1912).

the merchant seeking goodly pearls—all the merchant race, find the precious one they seek, and sell their all to buy it, they will make it theirs.

The question I began with—"How to be a Christian in trade?" is, I think, now sufficiently answered. . . . [I think it will be agreed] that there is no calling in which a christian may grow faster, and rise higher in all holy attainments. After he has once learned how to enjoy God in his calling, how to carry Christ directly into his works, and do all in the higher consciousness of Christ revealed, his satisfactions will be great, his increase rapid, his strength immovable, and his very sleep elysian. And what is a nobler sight to look upon, than a christian merchant, standing at the head of his operations; thriving in the small, or rolling up his immense income in the large; doing every thing squarely, as in terms of business, and not in a fast and loose manner, yet with a christian heart as flexible and free, and as little hampered by the mechanism of trade, as love itself must ever be; then passing out among his kind, to look about for objects wanting his aid; standing as a bank of charity for all good necessities to draw upon; resorted to with confidence by all who are forward in good works; spreading his generosity well up toward the limit of his surplus means; firm in credit; honored for his word of promise; sought unto in trust by the righteous, and remembered in the prayers of the poor—is there on this earth a character more to be envied, or more genuinely Christ-like than he?

# From *Women's Suffrage:*
## *The Reform Against Nature* (1869)*

[N]o argument for women's suffrage, based on the equality, or equally human property of women with men, can have more than a show of validity; for the reason that men and women are, to some very large extent, unlike in kind; and it may be so far unlike, as to forbid any rational comparison as respects equality; and, of course, to forbid any such inference of right for women because that right is accorded to men. It becomes, in this view, a matter of consequence to inquire whether the supposed unlikeness of kind includes matters of distinction that amount to a proper disqualification, or which really forbid, as contrary to nature, the extension of any such political right to women.

It is not to be denied that women are made in the image of God as truly as men, having faculties and categories of mind that are equal in number, and so far similar in kind, as to pass under the same general names. What is right and true to one sex, is right and true also to the other. They think by the same laws, they perceive, and judge, and remember, and will, and love, and hate, in the exercise of functions that compose personalities psychologically similar, however different in degree, and however differently tempered, fibered, tensified, and toned for action. In a word, they are equally human, and compared with orders of being above and below them are of the same kind. And yet in their relationship of sex, within their own human order, they are so widely different, nevertheless, that the distinction never misses observation. Their very personality, which even seemed identical in the inventory, taking on sexhood, becomes broadly differential in that fact, and submits to a deep-set, dual classification.

A mere glance at the two sexes, externally related, suggests some very wide distinction of mold whatever it be. The man is taller and more muscular, has a larger brain, and a longer stride in his walk. The woman is lighter and shorter, and moves more gracefully. In physical strength the man is greatly superior, and the base in his voice and the shag on his face, and the swing and sway of his shoulders, represent a personality in him that has some attribute of thunder. But there is no look of thunder in the

* [Ed.] *Women's Suffrage: The Reform Against Nature* (New York: Charles Scribner & Co., 1869). Dedicated to his wife. Included here: pp. 49–67.

woman. Her skin is too finely woven, too wonderfully delicate to be the rugged housing of thunder. Her soft, upper octave voice, her small hands, her features played as in quality and not for quantity, her complexion played as if there were a principle of beauty living under it—there is abundance of expression here, as many great, proud souls of heroes have been finding in all ages, but it is unOlympic as possible in kind. Glancing thus upon man, his look says, Force, Authority, Decision, Self-asserting Counsel, Victory. And the woman as evidently says, "I will trust, and be cherished and give sympathy and take ownership in the victor, and double his honors by the honors I contribute myself." They are yet one species, but if they were two, they would be scarcely more unlike. So very wide is the unlikeness, that they are a great deal more like two species, than like two varieties. Their distinction of sex puts them in different classes of being, only they are classes so nearly unified by their unlikeness, that they compose a whole, so to speak, of humanity, by their common relationship. One is the force principle, the other is the beauty principle. One is the forward, pioneering mastery, the out-door battle-ax of public war and family providence; the other is the indoor faculty, *covert*, as the law would say, and complementary, mistress and dispenser of the enjoyabilities. Enterprise and high counsel belong to one, also to batter the severities of fortune, conquer the raw material of supply; ornamentation, order, comfortable use, all flavors, and garnishes, and charms to the other. The man, as in fatherhood, carries the name and flag; the woman, as in motherhood, takes the name on herself and puts it on her children, passing out of sight legally, to be a covert nature included henceforth in her husband. They are positivity and receptivity, they are providence and use, they are strength and beauty, they are mass and color, they are store-house and table, they are substance and relish, and nothing goes to its mark or becomes a real value till it passes both.

But we are dealing, so far, in this outward delineation of the sexual distinctions, in matters general, and have not taken up, as yet, the more particular matter at issue in our question of suffrage. The precise point here to be observed, is that masculinity carries, in the distribution of sex, the governmental function. The forwarding force, the brave-and-dare element, whether toward nature or against human opposers, the responsible engineering of place and work and calling, all determinations outward, whether toward enemies, or among causes, or in ventures of commerce, or in diplomatic treaties and warlike relations of peoples, belong to man and to what may be called his manly prerogative. That is, man is to govern; all government belongs to men. Not that women are never set in kingly positions to present, or personate the kingly power; of that I shall speak hereafter in another place. For the present, I simply remark, that the authority they wield in such cases is only what the masculine traditions put upon them, or into them, when they are used to fill the gaps of kinghood, by maintaining the court pageantries and the royal signature; they do not reign as kings do by an authority that is largely personal in themselves. Were they obliged to maintain themselves in that way, it would very soon be discovered how little authority there is in women. We take pleasure not seldom in allowing women to rule us by the volunteering deference we pay to their womanhood; we often talk of our loyalty to the sex; but we never see the woman who can hold a particle of authority in us by her own positive rule or the emphasis of her own personality. . . .

Asserting in this very decisive manner the natural submission of women, and their very certain lack, whether as respects the right or the fact, of authority, it will seem to many, as I very much fear, to be a harsh, or even a rude and coarse attack upon their sex. If it is so taken, it certainly need not be. We Americans take up some very crude notions of subordination, as if it implied inferior quality, character, power. No such thing is true, or less than plainly false. Subordination is one thing, inferiority an immensely different thing. Subordinate as they are, in their naturally sheltered relation, I seriously doubt whether we should not also assert their superiority. They do quite as much, and I strongly suspect, more for the world. Their moral nature is more delicately perceptive. Their religious inspirations, or inspirabilities, put them closer to God, as having a more celestial property and affinities more superlative. It may be that men have larger quantity in the scale of talent, while yet they are enough coarser in the grain of their quality to more than balance the score. . . .

But there is an aspect of privilege, in this matter of subordination, which, instead of inferring the inferiority of women, gives them, when morally considered, the truest and sublimest conditions of ascendency. The highest virtues, purest in motive and really most difficult, are never to be looked for in the most forward and potentially regnant states. They belong rather to the subject conditions, where the coarse admixtures of pride and worldly power are shut away. We get the true analogy here in the great domain of nature, where the coarse and forceful causes seem to be doing every thing, and yet, in all finest, truest estimates of power, do comparatively nothing. The sun blazes and burns, the volcanoes burst and bury cities with ashes, the earthquakes rock and rend, the comets blaze on the sky, and the fierce windstorms tear it; and these and such like make up, as we think, the supreme causes to which all the humblest ingredients of our landscapes are of course inferior. And yet, if we come to the true scale of honors gotten upon human feeling, or in it, these same humbler, these inferior things of the landscapes are, in fact, immensely superior, and the others have but a hundredth part of the significance. The dews, the grasses, the green life of the trees, the fragrant breath of the mornings, the sunset colors on the clouds and the hills, the springs that break out under them, and the brooks leaping down their slopes, the songs of the birds, the feeding of cattle in their pastures—the inventory is a long one; who can tell what is in it, or how much? This only we know, that the great world-forces holding sway and swinging above are scarcely appreciable, in comparison with the finer things of beauty they subordinate. We do not half as much respect or feel the dominating forces of the world as we do the dominated graces. Or if certain gross, coarse-judging souls, will think great things are done for them only by causes that bruise and batter, and that other things subordinate to these are of course inferior, these latter still will not be inferior even to them. After all, the woman things of the world, the patient-working, unobtrusive, graceful causes will be doing more.

Under this analogy, we perceive how force, by its own nature, always and of course subordinates beauty. And it is just as true in things moral and spiritual as in things natural. Only they that are humble can be exalted; only the last can be first. The highest, finest molds of good, are grown only in the lowliest and most subject conditions. Was Mary inferior because she was a lowly, subject woman? Was her holy thing, her son, inferior because he was subject, in his beautiful childhood, and subject all his life long, down to the last hour's breath and the last nail driven? Many have imagined that they discovered in Jesus both a manly and a womanly nature, and that he became the perfect one, because in this union he was able, in so great force and authority, to bear so many things with a gentle submission and an unfaltering patience.

There can not, in this view, be a greater mistake, or one that indicates a coarser apprehension, than when our women, agitating for the right of suffrage, take it as an offense against their natural equality, that they are not allowed to help govern the world. It is as if the gentle mignonnette and violet were raised in protest against the regal dahlia, when they are in truth a great deal more potentially regnant themselves. What do these women ask, in fact, but to be weighed in the gross weight-scales of force, making nothing of that higher, finer nature, by which God expects it of them to flavor the world. They must govern, they must go into the fight, they must bruise and batter themselves— what are they equal to, if they are not equal to men? As if it were nothing, a little way back, after all the coarse things of the world are done, to govern, by graces, the men that govern by forces, and go through family and country, and the times, with a ministry more powerful, finer in the motive, less mixed with selfishness and will, and just as much closer to the really celestial type of good. God save us from the loss of this better, almost divinely superior ministry; for lost it will assuredly be, when our women have come down to be litigators with us in the candidacies, contests, and campaigns of political warfare. Still life is then no more, and the man who goes home at night from his caucus fight, or campaign speech, goes in, not to cease and rest, but to be dinned with the echo, or perhaps bold counter-echo of his own harsh battle. The kitchen dins the parlor, and one end of the table dins the other. Upstairs, down-stairs, in the lady's chamber—every where the same harsh gong is ringing, from year to year. Oh! if we could get away! how many will then say it, and pray it—into some bright corner where yet there are true women left—women with soft voices, shrilled by no brassiness or dinging sound of party war!

Why, if our women could but see what they are doing now, what superior grades of beauty and power they fill, and how far above equality with men they rise, when they keep their own pure atmosphere of silence, and their field of peace, how they make a realm into which the poor bruised fighters, with their passions galled, and their minds scarred with wrong—their hates, disappointments, grudges, and hard-worn ambitions—may come in, to be quieted, and civilized, and get some touch of the angelic, I think they would be very little apt to disrespect their womanly subordination. It will signify any thing but their inferiority. If they are already taken with the foolish ambition of place, or of winning a public name, they may not be satisfied. But in that case they barter for this honor a great deal more than they can rightly spare. God's highest honors never go with noise, but they wait on silent worth, on the consciousness of good, on secret charities, and ministries untainted by ambition. Could they but say to the noisy nothings of this bribery, "Get thee hence, Satan," as Christ did to the same coarse nonsense of flattery, they would keep their subject-way of life as he kept his, and would think it honor enough that they also came not to be ministered unto, but to minister. And if it be the question for them, whether it is better to be classed in privilege with Jesus the subject, or with Caesar the sovereign, it should not be difficult to decide.

Thus far we go in the principle that women are made to be subordinate, and men to be the forward operators and dominating authorities of the world. They have another field, where their really finer qualities and more inspirable gifts may get full room and scope for the most effective and divinest offices of life. Indeed we do not evenly set the balance of the question, if we do not say that woman has her government as truly as man, only it is not political, not among powers, and laws, and public causes. He governs from without downward, and she from within upward, and though there be a great difference of kind between our two words master and mistress, using this latter in its true, good sense, there is not a whit more of control signified, when we say that the man is the mastering power of the woman, than that she is the mistressing power of the man. He is at a point of sway more coarse, direct, and absolute—more nearly akin to force. She is at a point where she captivates the force, by a beautiful and right enjoyment of it, takes possession of the man, property, and soul, and will, and calling, and makes him joyfully her own. If the cases were inverted, he would make a coarse, awkward figure doubtless in the mistressing kind of government; but if we are to agitate for equality, why should he not have the beautiful chance given him of being a mistress-power in life—on the score of equality, even as she obtains a mastering power in life, when she obtains the suffrage.

As regards this right of priority and pioneering headship in man, and the so far subordinate and subject state in woman, implying still no superiority in him, and more than possible superiority in her, we have another illustration furnished by religion, that to such as have a true insight of the Christian plan or economy, will be strikingly apt and impressive. I refer to what is called the *law* and the *gospel*, as mutually related to each other. The law, which is the man, goes before, rough-hewing the work of the government. It is Sinai-like, and speaks in thunder. It commands, and, by sanctions of force, where force is wanted, vindicates its own supreme authority. It so far has priority in rule, that it never can have any thing less; for the cessation of law is the cessation of government, and if it should only fall into second place or equal place with any thing else, it would lose the inherent sovereignty of its nature, when, of course, in can be law no longer. The gospel, meantime coming after in order is the woman. It is subject as gospel to the husband, that is, to the law; it is made under the law; and the whole historic operation, by which it is organized, is itself obedience, submission, love, and sacrifice. And it is so perfectly subject to the law, that it professes nothing but a fulfillment of the law, and a universal recovery to it. Setting up for equality with law, or for itself, as having good right to assert and advance itself, is never so much as thought of; if it can but write the law on the heart of transgressors, all its wifely ends or ambitions are answered. And this it is supposed to do, by what is called grace; that is, by a way of approach so gentle, so winsome, and lovely, and close to the manner of true womanly grace, as to be another, more effective, side of the divine power; that which is the power of God unto salvation.

And now suppose the question to be raised, which of these is superior—works in the highest talent, does the greatest things, takes largest hold of the future, bears the loftiest inspirations, has most beauty of God in it, and really displays the finest, most etherealizing power? Undoubtedly it is the gospel. It goes above the law in doing every thing for it, and overtops it in glory, by submission to it. No power is in it, but the power of suffering and a subject state. It lives in sorrow and dies in sacrifice, and accomplishes just what the law, in "that it was weak," could not accomplish. The coarse ideas of force, and majesty, and all the pomps and thunders of enforcement are omitted here, and the simple wifehood of God's love, and beauty, is revealed, by what is lowliest and most dejected. And this is grace, the world-transforming grace in which God's empire culminates.

And yet our women will not have their subordinate or subject state, because it makes them inferior! They want, alas! the culture of soul that is wanted to see the superiority to which they are elected. They come in the wedding grace of their Cana, or the suffering grace of their Calvary, and insist on their right to be Sinai, and play the thunders too themselves. "Give us also power," they say; and power to them is force, or an equal right of command. A most miserable and really low misconception, if only they had grace to see it. Here is their true power, in a disinterested and subject life of good. And there is a way in this to govern men, that is greatness itself and victory. What can the woman do that wants to vote, in order to be somewhat, but fume, and chafe, and tear, under what she calls the wrongs of her husband—so to make her weakness more weak, and her defeat more miserable—when if she could only consent to be true gospel and woman together, to be gentle, and patient, and right, and fearless, how certainly would she come out superior and put him at her feet. There seems to me, in this view, I confess, to be something sacred, or angelic, in such womanhood. The morally grandest sight we see in this world is a real and ideally true woman. Send her to the polls if you will, give her an office, set the Hon. before her name, and by that time she is nobody.

# From "Our Obligations to the Dead" (1865)*

BRETHREN OF THE ALUMNI:—

To pay fit honors to our dead is one of the fraternal and customary offices of these anniversies; never so nearly an office of high public duty as now, when we find the roll of our membership starred with so many names made sacred by the giving up of life for the Republic. We knew them here in terms of cherished intimacy; some of them so lately that we scarcely seem to have been parted from them; others of them we have met here many times, returning to renew, with us, their tender and pleasant recollections of the past; but we meet them here no more: they are gone to make up their hecatomb offered for their and our great nation's life. Hence it has been specially desired on this occasion, that we honor their heroic sacrifice by some fit remembrance. . . .

There are various ways in which a people, delivered by great struggles of war, may endeavor to pay their testimony of honor to the men who have fallen. They may do it by chanting requiems for the repose of their souls; which, though it may not have any great effect in that precise way, is at least an act of implied homage and gratitude. The same thing is attempted more frequently by covering the dead benefactors and heroes with tributes of eulogy; only here it is a disappointment, that none but a few leaders are commemorated, while the undistinguished multitude, who jeoparded their lives most freely, are passed by and forgot. The best thing therefore to be done, worthiest both of the dead and the living, is, it seems to me, that which I now propose,—to recount our obligations to the dead in general; what they have done for us, what they have earned at our hands, and what they have put it on us to do for the dear common country to which they sold their life. . . .

[A]ccording to the true economy of the world, so many of its grandest and most noble benefits have and are to have a tragic origin, and to come as outgrowths only of blood. Whether it be that sin is in the world, and the whole creation groaneth in the necessary throes of its demonized life, we need not stay to inquire; for sin would be in the world and the demonizing spell would be upon it. Such was, and was to be, and is, the

* [Ed.] An oration in honor of Yale alumni who died in the Civil War. Published in *Building Eras in Religion* (New York: Charles Scribners Sons, 1881), pp. 319–55. Included here: pp. 319–21, 325–42, 349–55.

economy of it. Common life, the world's great life, is in the large way tragic. As the mild benignity and peaceful reign of Christ begins at the principle: "without shedding of blood, there is no remission," so, without shedding of blood, there is almost nothing great in the world, or to be expected for it. For the life is in the blood,—all life; and it is put flowing within, partly for the serving of a nobler use in flowing out on fit occasion, to quicken and consecrate whatever it touches. God could not plan a Peace-Society world, to live in the sweet amenities, and grow great and happy by simply thriving and feeding. There must be bleeding also. Sentiments must be born that are children of thunder; there must be heroes and heroic nationalities, and martyr testimonies, else there will be only mediocrities, insipidities, common-place men, and common-place writings,—a sordid and mean peace, liberties without a pulse, and epics that are only eclogues.

And there it is that the dead of our war have done for us a work so precious, which is their own,—they have bled for us; and by this simple sacrifice of blood they have opened for us a new great chapter of life. We were living before in trade and commerce, bragging of our new cities and our census reports, and our liberties that were also consciously mocked by our hypocrisies; having only the possibilities of great inspirations and not the fact, materialized more and more evidently in our habits and sentiments, strong principally in our discords and the impetuosity of our projects for money. But the blood of our dead has touched our souls with thoughts more serious and deeper, and begotten, as I trust, somewhat of that high-bred inspiration which is itself the possibility of genius, and of a true public greatness. Saying nothing then for the present of our victors and victories, let us see what we have gotten by the blood of our slain.

And first of all, in this blood our unity is cemented and forever sanctified. Something was gained for us here, at the beginning, by our sacrifices in the fields of our Revolution,—something, but not all. Had it not been for this common bleeding of the States in their common cause, it is doubtful whether our Constitution could ever have been carried. The discords of the Convention were imminent, as we know, and were only surmounted by compromises that left them still existing. They were simply kenneled under the Constitution and not reconciled, as began to be evident shortly in the doctrines of state sovereignty, and state nullification, here and there asserted. We had not bled enough, as yet, to merge our colonial distinctions and make us a proper nation. Our battles had not been upon a scale to thoroughly mass our feeling, or gulf us in a common cause and life. Against the state-rights doctrines, the logic of our Constitution was decisive, and they were refuted a thousand times over. But such things do not go by argument. No argument transmutes a discord, or composes a unity where there was none. The matter wanted here was blood, not logic, and this we now have on a scale large enough to meet our necessity. True it is blood on one side, and blood on the other,—all the better for that; for bad bleeding kills, and righteous bleeding sanctifies and quickens. The state-rights doctrine is now fairly bled away, and the unity died for, in a way of such prodigious devotion, is forever sealed and glorified.

Nor let any one be concerned for the sectional relations of defeat and victory. For there has all the while been a grand, suppressed sentiment of country in the general field of the rebellion, which is bursting up already into sovereignty out of the soil itself. There is even a chance that this sentiment may blaze into a passion hot enough to utterly burn up whatever fire itself can master. At all events it will put under the ban, from this time forth, all such instigators of treason as could turn their peaceful States into hells of desolation, and force even patriotic citizens to fight against the homage they bore their country. However this may be, the seeds of a true public life are in the soil, waiting to grow apace. It will be as when the flood of Noah receded. For the righteous man perchance began to bethink himself shortly, and to be troubled, that he took no seeds into the ark; but no sooner were the waters down, than the oaks and palms and all great trees sprung into life, under the dead old trunks of the forest, and the green world reappeared even greener than before; only the sections had all received new seeds, by a floating exchange, and put them forthwith into growth together with their own. So the unity now to be developed, after this war-deluge is over, is even like to be more cordial than it ever could have been. It will be no more thought of as a mere human compact, or composition, always to be debated by the letter, but it will be that bond of common life which God has touched with blood; a sacredly heroic, Providentially tragic unity, where God's cherubim stand guard over grudges and hates and remembered jealousies, and the sense of nationality becomes even a kind of religion. How many would have said that the Saxon Heptarchy, tormented by so many intrigues and feuds of war, could never be a nation! But their formal combination under Egbert, followed by their wars against the Danes under Alfred, set them in a solid, sanctified unity, and made them, as a people, one true England, instead of the seven Englands that were; which seven were never again to be more than historically remembered. And so, bleeding on together from that time to this in all sorts of wars; wars civil and wars abroad, drenching the land and coloring the sea with their blood; gaining all sorts of victories and suffering all kinds of defeats; their parties and intestine strifes are no more able now to so much as raise a thought that is not in allegiance to their country. In like manner,—let no one doubt of it,—these United States, having dissolved the intractable matter of so many infallible theories and bones of contention in the dreadful menstruum of their blood, are to settle into fixed unity, and finally into a nearly homogeneous life.

Passing to another point of view, we owe it to our dead in this terrible war, that they have given us the possibility of a great consciousness and great public sentiments. There must needs be something lofty in a people's action, and above all something heroic in their sacrifices for a cause, to sustain a great sentiment in them. They will try, in the smooth days of peace and golden thriftiness and wide-spreading growth, to have it, and perhaps will think they really have it, but they will only have semblances and counterfeits; patriotic professions that are showy and thin, swells and protestations that are only oratorical and have no true fire. All the worse if they have interests and institutions that are all the while mocking their principles; breeding factions that can be quieted only by connivances and compromises and political bargains, that sell out their muniments of right and nationality. Then you shall see all high devotion going down as by a law, till nothing is left, but the dastard picture of a spent magistracy that, when every thing is falling into wreck, can only whimper that it sees not any thing it can do! Great sentiments go when they are not dismissed, and will not come when they are sent for. We cannot keep them by much talk, nor have them because we have heard of them and seen them in a classic halo. A lofty public consciousness arises only when things are loftily and nobly done. It is only when we are rallied by a cause, in that cause receive a great inspiration, in that inspiration give our bodies to the death, that at last, out of many such heroes dead, comes the possibility of great thoughts, fired by sacrifice, and a true public magnanimity.

In this view, we are not the same people that we were, and never can be again. Our young scholars, that before could only find the forms of great feeling in their classic studies, now catch the fire of it unsought. Emulous before of saying fine things for their country, they now choke for the impossibility of saying what they truly feel. The pitch of their life is raised. The tragic blood of the war is a kind of new capacity for them. They perceive what it is to have a country and a public devotion. Great aims are close at hand, and in such aims a finer type of manners. And what shall follow, but that, in their more invigorated, nobler life, they are seen hereafter to be manlier in thought and scholarship, and closer to genius in action.

I must also speak of the new great history sanctified by this war, and the blood of its fearfully bloody sacrifices. So much worth and character were never sacrificed in a human war before. And by this mournful offering, we have bought a really stupendous chapter of history. We had a little very beautiful history before, which we were beginning to cherish and fondly cultivate. But we had not enough of it to beget a full historic consciousness. As was just now intimated in a different way, no people ever become vigorously conscious, till they mightily do, and heroically suffer. The historic sense is close akin to tragedy. We say it accusingly often,—and foolishly,—that history cannot live on peace, but must feed itself on blood. The reason is that, without the blood, there is really nothing great enough in motive and action, taking the world as it is, to create a great people or story. If a gospel can be executed only in blood, if there is no power of salvation strong enough to carry the world's feeling which is not gained by dying for it, how shall a selfish race get far enough above itself, to be kindled by the story of its action in the dull routine of its common arts of peace? Doubtless it should be otherwise, even as goodness should be universal; but so it never has been, and upon the present footing of evil never can be. The great cause must be great as in the clashing of evil; and heroic inspirations, and the bleeding of heroic worth must be the zest of the story. Nations can sufficiently live only as they find how to energetically die. In this view, some of us have felt, for a long time, the want of a more historic life, to make us a truly great people. This want is now supplied; for now, at last, we may be said to have gotten a history. The story of this four years' war is the grandest chapter, I think, of heroic fact, and tragic devotion, and spontaneous public sacrifice, that has ever been made in our world. The great epic story of Troy is but a song in comparison. There was never a better, and never so great a cause; order against faction, law against conspiracy, liberty and right against the madness and defiant wrong of slavery, the unity and salvation of the greatest future nationality and freest government of the world, a perpetual state of war to be averted, and the preservation for mankind of an example of popular government and free society that is a token of promise for true manhood, and an omen of death to old abuse and prescriptive wrong the world over; this has been our cause, and it is some thing to say that we have borne ourselves worthily in it. Our noblest and best sons have given their life to it. We have dotted whole regions with battle-fields. We have stained how many rivers, and bays, and how many hundred leagues of railroad, with our blood! We have suffered appalling defeats; twice at Bull Run, at Wilson's Creek, in the great campaign of the Peninsula, at Cedar Mountain, at Fredericksburg, at Chancellorsville, at Chickamauga, and upon the Red River, leaving our acres of dead on all these fields and many others less conspicuous; yet, abating no jot of courage and returning with resolve unbroken, we have converted these defeats into only more impressive victories. In this manner too, with a better fortune nobly earned, we have hallowed, as names of glory and high victory, Pea Ridge, Donelson, Shiloh, Hilton Head, New Orleans, Vicksburg, Port Hudson, Stone River, Lookout Mountain, Resaca, Atlanta, Fort Fisher, Gettysburg, Nashville, Wilmington, Petersburg and Richmond, Bentonville, Mobile Bay, and, last of all, the forts of Mobile city. All these and a hundred others are now become, and in all future time are to be, names grandly historic. And to have them is to be how great a gift for the ages to come! By how many of the future children of the Republic will these spots be visited, and how many will return from their pilgrimages thither, blest in remembrances of the dead, to whom they owe their country! . . .

God forbid that any prudishness of modesty should here detain us. Let us fear no more to say that we have won a history and the right to be a consciously historic people. Henceforth our new world even heads the old, having in this single chapter risen clean above it. The wars of Caesar, and Frederic, and Napoleon, were grand enough in their leadership, but there is no grand people or popular greatness in them, consequently no true dignity. In this war of ours it is the people, moving by their own decisive motion, in the sense of their own great cause. For this cause we have volunteered by the million, and in three thousand millions of money, and by the resolute bleeding of our men and the equally resolute bleeding of our self-taxation, we have bought and sanctified consentingly all these fields, all that is grand in this thoroughly principled history.

Again, it is not a new age of history only that we owe to the bloody sacrifices of this war, but in much the same manner the confidence of a new literary age; a benefit that we are specially called, in such a place as this, and on such an occasion, to remember and fitly acknowledge. Great public throes are, mentally speaking, changes of base for some new thought-campaign in a people. Hence the brilliant new literature of the age of Queen Elizabeth; then of another golden era under Anne; and then still again, as in the arrival of another birth-time, after the Napoleonic wars of George the Fourth. The same thing has been noted, I believe, in respect to the wars of Greece and Germany. Only it is in such wars as raise the public sense and majesty of a people that the result is seen to follow. For it is the high-souled feeling raised that quickens high-souled thought, and puts the life of genius in the glow of new-born liberty. This we are now to expect, for the special reason also that we have here, for the first time, conquered a position. Thus it will be seen that no great writer becomes himself, in his full power, till he has gotten the sense of position. Much more true is this of a people. And here has been our weakness until now. We have held the place of cliency, we have taken our models and laws of criticism, and to a great extent our opinions, from the English motherhood of our language and mind. Under that kind of pupilage we live no longer; we are thoroughly weaned from it, and become a people in no secondary right. Henceforth we are not going to write English, but American. As we have gotten our position, we are now to have our own civilization, think our own thoughts, rhyme in our own measures, kindle our own fires, and make our own canons of criticism, even as we settle the proprieties of punishment for our own traitors. We are not henceforth to live as by cotton and corn and trade, keeping the downward slope of thrifty mediocrity. Our young men are not going out of college, staled, in the name of discipline, by their carefully conned lessons, to be launched on the voyage of life as ships without wind, but they are to have great sentiments, and mighty impulsions, and souls alive all through in fires of high devotion.

We have gotten also now the historic matter of a true oratoric inspiration, and the great orators are coming after. In the place of politicians we are going to have, at least, some statesmen; for we have gotten the pitch of a grand, new, Abrahamic statesmanship,* unsophisticated, honest and real; no cringing sycophancy, or cunning art of demagogy. We have also facts, adventures, characters enough now in store, to feed five hundred years of fiction. We have also plots, and lies, and honorable perjuries, false heroics, barbaric murders and assassinations, conspiracies of fire and poison,—enough of them, and wicked enough, to furnish the Satanic side of tragedy for long ages to come; coupled also with such grandeurs of public valor and principle, such beauty of heroic sacrifice, in womanhood and boyhood, as tragedy has scarcely yet been able to find. As to poetry, our battle-fields are henceforth names poetic, and our very soil is touched with a mighty poetic life. In the rustle of our winds, what shall the waking soul of our poets think of, but of brave souls riding by? In our thunders they may hear the shocks of charges, and the red of the sunset shall take a tinge in their feeling from the summits where our heroes fell. A new sense comes upon every thing, and the higher soul of mind, quickened by new possibilities, finds inspirations where before it found only rocks, and ploughlands, and much timber for the saw. Are there no great singers to rise in this new time? Are there no unwonted fires to be kindled in imaginations fanned by these new glows of devotion? We seem, as it were in a day, to be set in loftier ranges of thought, by this huge flood-tide that has lifted our nationality, gifted with new sentiments and finer possibilities, commissioned to create, and write, and sing, and, in the sense of a more poetic feeling at least, to be all poets. . . .

I might also speak at large, if I had time, of the immense benefit these dead have conferred upon our free institutions themselves, by the consecrating blood of their sacrifice. But I can only say that having taken the sword to be God's ministers, and to vindicate the law as his ordinance, they have done it even the more effectively in that they have died for it. It has been a wretched fault of our people that we have so

---

* [Ed.] The reference, of course, is to Abraham Lincoln.

nearly ignored the moral foundations of our government. Regarding it as a merely human creation, we have held it only by the tenure of convenience. Hence came the secession. For what we create by our will, may we not dissolve by the same? Bitter has been the cost of our pitifully weak philosophy. In these rivers of blood we have now bathed our institutions, and they are henceforth to be hallowed in our sight. Government is now become Providential,—no more a mere creature of our human will, but a grandly moral affair. The awful stains of sacrifice are upon it, as upon the fields where our dead battled for it, and it is sacred for their sakes. The stamp of God's sovereignity is also upon it; for he has beheld their blood upon its gate-posts and made it the sign of his passover. Henceforth we are not to be manufacturing government, and defying in turn its sovereignty because we have made it ourselves; but we are to revere its sacred rights, rest in its sacred immunities, and have it even as the Caesar whom our Christ himself requires us to obey. Have we not also proved, written it down for all the ages to come, that the most horrible, God-defying crime of this world is unnecessary rebellion?

I might also speak of the immense contribution made for religion, by the sacrifices of these bleeding years. Religion, at the first, gave impulse, and, by a sublime recompense of reaction, it will also receive impulse. What then shall we look for but a new era now to break forth, a day of new gifts and powers and holy endowments from on high, wherein great communities and friendly nations shall be girded in sacrifice, for the cause of Christ their Master? . . .

But there is one other and yet higher duty that we owe to these dead; viz., that we take their places and stand in their cause. It is even a great law of natural duty that the living shall come into the places and works of the dead. The same also is accepted and honored by Christianity, when it shows the Christian son, and brother, and friend, stepping into the places made vacant by the dead, to assume their blessed and great work unaccomplished, and die, if need be, in the testimony of a common martyrdom. They challenged, in this manner, if the commentators will suffer it, the vows of baptism, and "were baptized for the dead,"—consecrated upon the dead, for the work of the dead. God lays it upon us in the same way now, to own the bond of fealty that connects us with the fallen, in the conscious community and righteous kinship of their cause. And then, as brothers baptized for the dead,—Alumni, so to speak, of the Republic,—we are to execute their purpose and fulfill the idea that inspired them. Neither is it enough at this point to go off in a general heroic, promising, in high rhetoric, to give our life for the country in like manner. There is no present likelihood that we shall be called to do any such thing. No, but we have duties upon us that are closer at hand; viz., to wind up and settle this great tragedy in a way to exactly justify every drop of blood that has been shed in it. Like the blood of righteous Abel it cries both to us and to God, from every field, and river, and wood, and road, dotted by our pickets and swept by the march of our armies.

First of all we are sworn to see that no vestige of state sovereignty is left, and the perpetual, supreme sovereignty of the nation established. For what but this have our heroes died? Not one of them would have died for a government of mere optional continuance; not one for a government fit to be rebelled against. But they volunteered for a government in perfect right, and one to be perpetual as the stars, and they went to the death as against the crime of hell. . . .

One thing more we are also sworn upon the dead to do; viz., to see that every vestige of slavery is swept clean. We did not begin the war to extirpate slavery; but the war itself took hold of slavery on its way, and as this had been the gangrene of our wound from the first, we shortly put ourselves heartily to the cleansing, and shall not, as good surgeons, leave a part of the virus in it. We are not to extirpate the form and leave the fact. The whole black code must go; the law of passes, and the law of evidence, and the unequal laws of suit and impeachment for crime. We are bound, if possible, to make the emancipation work well; as it never can, till the old habit of domination, and the new grudges of exasperated pride and passion, are qualified by gentleness and consideration. Otherwise there will be no industry but only jangle; society in fact will be turned into a hell of poverty and confusion. And this kind relationship never can be secured, till the dejected and despised race are put upon the footing of men, and allowed to assert themselves somehow in the laws. Putting aside all theoretic notions of equality, and regarding nothing but the practical want of the emancipation, negro suffrage appears to be indispensable. . . .

Need I add, that now, by these strange fortunes of the rebellion rushing on its Providential overthrow, immense responsibilities are put upon us, that are new. A new style of industry is to be inaugurated. The soil is to be distributed over again, villages are to be created, schools established, churches erected, preachers and teachers provided, and money for these purposes to be poured out in rivers of benefaction, even as it has been in the war. A whole hundred years of new creation will be needed to repair these wastes and regenerate these habits of wrong; and we are baptized for the dead, to go forth in God's name, ceasing not, and putting it upon our children never to cease, till the work is done.

My task is now finished; only, alas! too feebly. There are many things I might say, addressing you as Alumni, as professors and teachers, and as scholars training here for the new age to come. But you will anticipate my suggestions, and pass on by me, to conceive a better wisdom for yourselves. One thing only I will name, which is fitting, as we part, for us all; viz., that without any particle of vain assumption, we swear by our dead to be Americans. Our position is gained! Our die of history is struck! Thank God we have a country, and that country has the chance of a future! Ours be it henceforth to cherish that country, and assert that future; also, to invigorate both by our own civilization, adorn them by our literature, consolidate them in our religion. Ours be it also, in God's own time, to champion, by land and sea, the right of this whole continent to be an American world, and to have its own American laws, and liberties, and institutions.

# SELECTED BIBLIOGRAPHY

I. Bushnell's Principal Works in Chronological Order.

["Natural Science and Moral Philosophy"]. A paper written in May 1832. MS Yale Divinity School Library.

A *Discourse on the Slavery Question*. Hartford: Case, Tiffany & Co., 1839. Pamphlet.

"Revelation." An address delivered in September 1839. MS Yale Divinity School Library.

*Barbarism the First Danger*. New York: n.p., 1847. Pamphlet; reprinted in the 1881 edition of *Work and Play*.

*Views of Christian Nurture and of Subjects Adjacent Thereto*. Hartford: Edwin Hunt, 1847; rpt. Delmar, N.Y.: Scholars Facsimiles & Reprints, 1975. (This book reprints Bushnell's *Discourses on Christian Nurture* (Boston, 1847) along with several other previously published articles and pamphlets.)

"Christ the Form of the Soul." A sermon written in February 1848. MS Yale Divinity School Library.

"Christian Comprehensiveness." *The New Englander* VI (January 1848), pp. 81–111.

*God in Christ*. Hartford: Brown and Parsons, 1849; rpt. New York: AMS Press, 1972.

*Christ in Theology*. Hartford: Brown & Parsons, 1851.

*Twentieth Anniversary: A Commemorative Discourse*. Hartford: Elihu Geer, 1853. Pamphlet.

*Nature and the Supernatural, as Together Constituting the One System of God*. New York: Charles Scribner, 1858; rpt. New York: AMS Press, 1973.

*Sermons for the New Life*. New York: Charles Scribner, 1858.

*Christian Nurture*. New York: Charles Scribner, 1861; rpt. New Haven: Yale University Press, 1967.

*Work and Play*. New York: Charles Scribner & Co., 1864. In the 1881 and 1903 editions, "Barbarism the First Danger" is substituted for "Agriculture in the East."

*Christ and His Salvation: in Sermons Variously Related Thereto*. New York: Charles Scribner & Co., 1865.

*The Vicarious Sacrifice, Grounded in Principles of Universal Obligation.* New York: Charles Scribner & Co., 1866; rpt. Hicksville, N.Y.: The Regina Press, 1974. In 1877, this work became Volume One of *The Vicarious Sacrifice Grounded in Principles Interpreted by Human Analogies* (New York: Charles Scriber's Sons).

*Moral Uses of Dark Things.* New York: Charles Scribner & Co., 1869.

"Our Gospel a Gift to the Imagination." *Hours at Home*, X (December 1869), pp. 159–72.

*Women's Suffrage; The Reform Against Nature.* New York: Charles Scribner & Co., 1869; rpt. Washington, D.C.: Zenger Publishing Co., Inc., 1978.

*Sermons on Living Subjects.* New York: Scribner, Armstrong & Co., 1872.

*Forgiveness and Law, Grounded in Principles Interpreted by Human Analogies.* New York: Scribner, Armstrong & Co., 1874; rpt. Hicksville, N.Y.: The Regina Press, 1974. In 1877, this work became Volume Two of *The Vicarious Sacrifice Grounded in Principles Interpreted by Human Analogies.* (New York: Charles Scribner's Sons).

*Building Eras in Religion.* New York: Charles Scribner's Sons, 1881.

*The Spirit in Man, Sermons and Selections.* New York: Charles Scribner's Sons, 1903.

## II. Useful Secondary Works.

Ahlstrom, Sydney E., ed. *Theology in America: The Major Protestant Voices from Puritanism to Neo-Orthodoxy.* Indianapolis: The Bobbs-Merrill Company, Inc., 1967.

Baird, Robert. "Horace Bushnell: A Romantic Approach to the Nature of Theology." *The Journal of Bible and Religion*, XXXIII (July 1965), pp. 229–40.

Bartlett, Irving H. "Bushnell, Cousin, and Comprehensive Christianity." *Journal of Religion*, XXXVII (1957), pp. 99–104.

*Bushnell Centenary: Minutes of the General Association of Connecticut.* Hartford: Hartford Press, the Case, Lockwood & Brainard Co., 1902.

Cheney, Mary Bushnell. *Life and Letters of Horace Bushnell.* New York: Harper & Brothers, 1880; rpt. New York: Arno Press, Inc., 1969.

Cherry, Conrad. *Nature and Religious Imagination: From Edwards to Bushnell.* Philadelphia: Fortress Press, 1980.

_____, "The Structure of Organic Thinking: Horace Bushnell's Approach to Language, Nature, and Nation." *Journal of the American Academy of Religion*, 40 (March 1972), pp. 3–20.

Clebsch, William A. *American Religious Thought: A History*. Chicago: The University of Chicago Press, 1973.

Cole, Charles G. "Horace Bushnell and the Slavery Question." *New England Quarterly*, XXIII (1950), pp. 19–30.

Crosby, Donald A. *Horace Bushnell's Theory of Language: In the Context of Other Nineteenth Century Philosophies of Language*. The Hague: Mouton, 1975.

Cross, Barbara. *Horace Bushnell: Minister to a Changing America*. Chicago: University of Chicago Press, 1958.

Douglas, Ann. *The Feminization of American Culture*. New York: Alfred A. Knopf, 1977.

Feidelson, Charles, Jr. *Symbolism and American Literature*. Chicago: University of Chicago Press, 1953.

Johnson, William A. *Nature and the Supernatural in the Theology of Horace Bushnell*. Lund: C.W.K. Gleerup, 1963.

Kirschenmann, Fred. "Horace Bushnell: Orthodox or Sabellian?" *Church History*, XXXIII (March 1964), pp. 49–59.

Lewis R.W.B. *The American Adam: Innocence, Tragedy, and Tradition in the Nineteenth Century*. Chicago: University of Chicago Press, 1955.

Munger, Theodore Thornton. *Horace Bushnell: Preacher and Theologian*. Boston: Houghton, Mifflin & Co., 1889.

Smith, David L. *Symbolism and Growth: The Religious Thought of Horace Bushnell*. AAR Dissertation Series 36. Chico, CA: Scholars Press, 1981.

Smith, H. Shelton. *Changing Conceptions of Original Sin: A Study in American Theology Since 1750*. New York: Charles Scribner's Sons, 1958.

_____, ed. *Horace Bushnell*. New York: Oxford University Press, 1965.

Stephens, Bruce M. *God's Last Metaphor: The Doctrine of the Trinity in New England Theology*. AAR Studies in Religion 24. Chico, CA: Scholars Press, 1981.

Weeks, Lewis. "Horace Bushnell on Black America." *Religious Education*, 68 (1973), pp. 28–41.

Welch, Claude. *Protestant Thought in the Nineteenth Century. Volume I, 1799–1870*. New Haven: Yale University Press, 1972.